BBC good food

ULTIMATE SLOW COOKER RECIPES

EDITOR
Sara Buenfeld

BOOKS

10 9 8 7 6

BBC Books, an imprint of Ebury Publishing
20 Vauxhall Bridge Road,
London SW1V 2SA

BBC Books is part of the Penguin Random
House group of companies whose
addresses can be found at
global.penguinrandomhouse.com

Photographs © BBC Magazines 2016
Recipes © BBC Worldwide 2016
Book design © Woodlands Books Ltd 2016
All recipes contained in this book first
appeared in BBC *Good Food* magazine.

First published by BBC Books in 2016

www.eburypublishing.co.uk

A CIP catalogue record for this book is
available from the British Library

ISBN 9781785941641

Printed and bound in Italy by Printer Trento

Project editor: Charlotte Macdonald
Design: Interstate Creative Partners Ltd
and Kathryn Gammon
Cover Design: Interstate Creative Partners Ltd
Production: Alex Goddard
Picture Researcher: Gabby Harrington

Penguin Random House is committed to a
sustainable future for our business, our readers
and our planet. This book is made from Forest
Stewardship Council® certified paper.

PICTURE AND RECIPE CREDITS

BBC Books would like to thank the following
people for providing photos. While every
effort has been made to trace and
acknowledge all photographers, we should
like to apologise should there be any errors or
omissions.

David Munns 9, 25, 27, 55, 57, 61, 63, 81, 97, 87,
107, 115, 125, 127, 135, 147, 165, 181,185, 193,197,
203, 219, 223, 269, 291; Gareth Morgans 33, 45,
67, 69, 95, 99, 109, 117, 143, 149, 179, 221, 225,
237, 249, 285; Lis Parsons 11, 17, 53, 65, 91, 119,
161, 169, 173, 211, 229, 245, 261, 289, 303, 309,
311; Myles New 19, 35, 39, 51, 83, 105, 167, 189,
191, 205, 247, 263, 253, 295, 275, 277; Stuart
Ovenden 37, 41, 79, 103, 121, 145, 187, 207, 209,
233, 241, 257, 317; Martin Brigdale 13; Sam
Stowell 15, 47, 89, 171, 255, 293; Charlie
Richards 21; Maja Smend 23, 177, 195, 279, 301;
Phillip Webb 29, 71, 93, 129, 281, 287, 313, 305;
Rob Streeter 31, 73, 75, 85; Will Heap 43, 101,
153, 155, 157, 137, 175, 239, 251, 227, 259, 265,
297, 299; Howard Shooter 271; Jean Cazals 49;
Toby Scott 77 213; Peter Cassidy 113, 131, 123,
151, 159, 199, 217, 243, 273, 283; Adrian
Lawrence 133; John Whitaker 139, 315; Ian
Wallace 307; Craig Robertson 141; David
Loftus 183.

All the recipes in this book were created by
the editorial team at *Good Food* and by
regular contributors to BBC Magazines.

Contents

INTRODUCTION 4

CHAPTER 1: Soups & starters 6

CHAPTER 2: Family favourites 58

CHAPTER 3: Casseroles, spicy stews & curries 110

CHAPTER 4: Easy entertaining 162

CHAPTER 5: Vegetarian & vegetables 214

CHAPTER 6: Puddings & preserves 266

INDEX 318

Introduction

Whether you are out all day and want to come home to a hot home-cooked meal, or you like to effortlessly entertain, using a slow cooker is a fantastic and energy-saving way to cook.

Slow cookers are increasing in popularity and we know that from the success of our previous slow cooker books, and the many requests we receive for recipes and advice.

Here we have brought together a collection of fabulous recipes from two previous best-selling books as well as new *Good Food* recipes that we have adapted and tested, to show you how versatile a slow cooker can be. It can also be an asset in the kitchen to help you part-cook conventional recipes like pies and cobblers or pasta dishes and pulled pork.

We have included family recipes like chilli con carne, chicken casserole and cottage pie, but also authentic curries and exotic dishes that you can enjoy with friends when you can spend a little more time in the kitchen. There are also preserves, gently cooked fish dishes, impressive desserts – even a Christmas pudding so that you don't have to worry about it steaming on the hob any more.

To get the best flavours from the ingredients, we found that it is better for many recipes to pre-fry meat and onions rather than put them in raw, but if you would rather get the recipe ready the night before, just cook from cold and add 1-2 hours to our cooking time to build in the heating process. Check manufacturer's instructions for advice too.

Many people who love to cook, love their slow cookers for the unique way that they cook, so plug in yours and see what you can do. We think you will be pleasantly surprised.

Getting the best from your slow cooker

Every slow cooker is different, so make sure you keep your manufacturer's manual handy when using it. However, here we'll share with you the *Good Food* team's top tips for slow cooking.

- Lots of the recipes can be changed to fit in with your lifestyle, so follow your manual's guidelines on decreasing or increasing cooking times by changing the temperature of the slow cooker. However, we've found rice and pasta dishes really work best when cooked on High for the shortest time possible.
- Always use easy-cook rice, if you can get it, and don't forget to rinse the rice well first. The more starch you can wash off the rice, the better the finished dish.
- Slow cookers vary considerably in size, so we've written a variety of recipes, for a variety of portions. Many of these are easily halved or doubled – check the individual recipes for recommendations.
- If the sauce of a stew or a casserole is a little thin for your liking, mix 1 tablespoon cornflour to a paste with a splash of the sauce, then transfer to a pan with a ladleful of the sauce and bring to the boil to thicken. Stir back into the stew and repeat if need be.
- If you want to adapt your own recipes to suit a slow cooker, look for something similar in this book and copy the timings – but reduce the liquid in your original recipe by around a third.

Sara

Sara Buenfeld

Notes & Conversion Tables

NOTES ON THE RECIPES

- Eggs are large in the UK and Australia and extra large in America unless stated.
- Wash fresh produce before preparation.
- Recipes contain nutritional analyses for 'sugar', which means the total sugar content including all natural sugars in the ingredients, unless otherwise stated.

APPROXIMATE LIQUID CONVERSIONS

Metric	Imperial	AUS	US
50ml	2fl oz	¼ cup	¼ cup
125ml	4fl oz	½ cup	½ cup
175ml	6fl oz	¾ cup	¾ cup
225ml	8fl oz	1 cup	1 cup
300ml	10fl oz/½ pint	½ pint	1¼ cups
450ml	16fl oz	2 cups	2 cups/1 pint
600ml	20fl oz/1 pint	1 pint	2½ cups
1 litre	35fl oz/1¾ pints	1¾ pints	1 quart

APPROXIMATE WEIGHT CONVERSIONS

- All the recipes in this book list both metric and imperial measurements. Conversions are approximate and have been rounded up or down. Follow one set of measurements only; do not mix the two.
- Cup measurements, which are used in Australia and America, have not been listed here as they vary from ingredient to ingredient. Kitchen scales should be used to measure dry/solid ingredients.

OVEN TEMPERATURES

GAS	°C	°C FAN	°F	OVEN TEMP.
¼	110	90	225	Very cool
½	120	100	250	Very cool
1	140	120	275	Cool or slow
2	150	130	300	Cool or slow
3	160	140	325	Warm
4	180	160	350	Moderate
5	190	170	375	Moderately hot
6	200	180	400	Fairly hot
7	220	200	425	Hot
8	230	210	450	Very hot
9	240	220	475	Very hot

SPOON MEASURES

Spoon measurements are level unless otherwise specified.
- 1 teaspoon (tsp) = 5ml
- 1 tablespoon (tbsp) = 15ml
- 1 Australian tablespoon = 20ml (cooks in Australia should measure 3 teaspoons where 1 tablespoon is specified in a recipe)

Good Food is concerned about sustainable sourcing and animal welfare. Where possible, humanely reared meats, sustainably caught fish (see fishonline.org for further information from the Marine Conservation Society) and free-range chickens and eggs are used when recipes are originally tested.

Chapter 1:

SOUPS & STARTERS

Moroccan Harira & Chicken Soup

Good for you and tasty too, this thick soup can easily be served as a filling supper or casual weekend lunch with toast and houmous.

 3-4 hours 4-5

- 3 tbsp olive oil, plus extra to drizzle
- 4 boneless, skinless chicken thighs
- 1 leek, washed and finely sliced
- 4 fat celery sticks, chopped into small pieces
- 3 large carrots, chopped into small pieces
- 2 big parsnips, peeled and chopped into small pieces
- small pack coriander, stalks finely chopped, leaves reserved to serve
- 1 tbsp cumin seeds
- 2 tsp each ground cumin, coriander, cinnamon and turmeric
- 2 tbsp harissa (we used Belazu)
- 2 x 400g cans chopped tomatoes
- 2 chicken stock cubes, crumbled
- 85g/3oz dried green lentils
- zest and juice 1 lemon
- 1 tbsp golden caster sugar
- natural yogurt, to serve (optional)

1 Heat the slow cooker if necessary. Heat half the oil in a frying pan, season the thighs and brown really well on both sides. Remove to a plate. Tip a mug of water into the pan and simmer, scraping up all the browned bits. Tip this liquid into a measuring jug for later.

2 Put the remaining oil, the vegetables and coriander stalks in a big saucepan. Gently cook until the veg is softened about 5 mins. Stir in the spices, turn up the heat, and cook for a few mins. Stir in the harissa, followed by the tomatoes, the chicken, stock cubes and lentils. Top up your jug of chickeny juices to 500ml/18fl oz with water, then add this, too. Bring to a simmer, then tip into the slow cooker, cover and cook for 2-3 hours until the vegetables are tender.

3 Lift the chicken from the soup and shred finely using a couple of forks. (The chicken will be very tender, so stirring the soup may well break it up for you instead.) Return to the soup with the lemon zest and juice and sugar, and season to taste. Ladle into bowls and top with a dollop of yogurt and the coriander leaves.

PER SERVING (5) 316 kcals, fat 14g, saturates 3g, carbs 28g, sugars 17g, fibre 7g, protein 22g, salt 1.6g

Roast Chicken Soup

Make this with leftovers from the Sunday roast, or simply poach a couple of chicken breasts in the slow cooker first, following the manufacturer's instructions.

 3-4 hours 4

- 1 tbsp olive oil
- 2 onions, chopped
- 3 medium carrots, chopped
- 1 tbsp thyme leaves, roughly chopped
- 1 litre/1¾ pints chicken stock
- 300g/10oz leftover roast chicken or poached chicken, shredded, or 1 roasted chicken carcass
- 200g/7oz frozen peas
- 3 tbsp Greek yogurt
- 1 garlic clove, crushed
- squeeze lemon juice
- crusty bread, to serve

1 Heat the slow cooker if necessary and heat the oil in a large heavy-based pan. Add the onions, carrots and thyme, then gently fry for 15 mins. Tip the veg into the slow cooker pot with the stock. If you're using a chicken carcass, add it now, breaking it in half if you need to. Cover and cook for 2–3 hours on High until the vegetables are tender.

2 If you used a carcass, remove it now, and shred any remaining chicken off the bones. Stir this back into the soup, or add your leftover shredded chicken, if using that instead, plus the peas, and cover and cook for 30 mins more.

3 Remove half the mixture, then purée with a stick blender (or ladle half the mixture into a blender or food processor and purée that). Tip back into the pot and check for seasoning.

4 Mix the yogurt, garlic and lemon juice, swirl into the soup in bowls, then serve with some crusty bread.

PER SERVING 339 kcals, fat 13g, saturates 3g, carbs 18g, sugars 11g, fibre 13g, protein 39g, salt 2.0g

Winter Leek & Potato Soup

If you are looking for an easy starter you won't go wrong with this delicate, creamy soup. It is quite rich, so ideal to serve in small portions.

 3 hours 6

- 50g/2oz butter
- 450g/1lb potatoes, cut into chunks
- 1 onion, chopped
- 450g/1lb leeks (the weight once the tops and outer leaves are trimmed), sliced
- 1 chicken or vegetable stock cube
- 150ml pot double cream
- milk, to taste

TO SERVE (OPTIONAL)
- knob of butter
- the white part of 1 leek, finely shredded
- snipped chives

1. Heat the slow cooker if necessary. Put the butter, potatoes, onion and leeks in a large pan and crumble in the stock cube. Pour in 500ml/18fl oz boiling water and bring to the boil.
2. Tip into the slow cooker, cover and cook on Low for 2½ hours until the vegetables are tender.
3. Add the cream (if garnishing use three-quarters of the pot) and blitz with a stick blender until silky smooth. Season and dilute with milk - you will need approx 50ml/2fl oz.
4. If garnishing the soup, keep it hot while you heat the butter in a small pan, add the leek and cook until softened. Spoon the soup into bowls, top with a swirl of the reserved cream, leek and chives, then grind over some pepper.

PER SERVING 252 kcals, fat 18 g, saturates 11g, carbs 18g, sugars 3g, fibre 3g, protein 5g, salt 0.7g

Spiced Carrot & Lentil Soup

If you've got a very large slow cooker it's worth making a double batch of this low-fat, super-healthy soup as it freezes beautifully.

 3½ hours   4    easily doubled

- 2 tsp cumin seeds
- pinch dried chilli flakes
- 2 tbsp olive oil
- 600g/1lb 5oz carrots, washed and coarsely grated (no need to peel)
- 140g/5oz red split lentils
- 700ml/1¼ pints hot vegetable stock
- 125ml/4fl oz milk
- plain yogurt and warmed naan breads, to serve

1 Heat the slow cooker if necessary. Put half the cumin seeds, half the chilli flakes, the oil, carrots, lentils and stock in the pot. Cover and cook on High for 3 hours until the lentils are tender.
2 Dry-fry the remaining cumin seeds and chilli flakes just until fragrant.
3 When the lentils are done, stir in the milk and whizz the soup with a stick blender or in a food processor until smooth (or leave it chunky, if you prefer). Add a splash of water if the soup is a bit thick for you. Season to taste and finish with a dollop of yogurt and a sprinkling of the toasted spices. Serve with warmed naan breads.

PER SERVING 238 kcals, fat 7g, saturates 1g, carbs 34g, sugars 5g, fibre 5g, protein 11g, salt 0.25g

Sweetcorn & Smoked Haddock Chowder

The perfect lunch for two, just add some fresh crusty bread and butter, and let the slow cooker do most of the work.

 4 hours 2  easily doubled

- knob of butter
- 2 rashers streaky bacon, chopped
- 1 onion, finely chopped
- 350g/12oz potatoes, cut into small cubes
- 500ml/18fl oz full-fat milk
- 140g/5oz sweetcorn, frozen or from a can
- 300g/10oz smoked haddock fillets, skinned
- chopped parsley, to garnish (optional)

1 Heat the slow cooker if necessary. Melt the butter in a frying pan. Tip in the bacon, onion and potatoes, then fry gently until the onion is soft. Scrape everything into the slow cooker pot with the milk. Cover and cook on High for 3 hours until the potatoes are tender.

2 Stir in the sweetcorn, sit the fish fillets on top and press down so they sit just under the surface of the liquid. Cover and cook for another 20–30 mins until the fish flakes easily when pressed.

3 Turn off the slow cooker pot and carefully lift the fish out and on to a plate. Flake into large chunks, checking for bones and discarding them as you go. Gently stir the fish back into the chowder, season with some black pepper. Scatter over the parsley, if using, and serve with plenty of crusty bread.

PER SERVING 550 kcals, fat 16g, saturates 7g, carbs 59g, sugars 18g, fibre 4g, protein 47g, salt 3.5g

Split Pea & Green Pea Smoked-ham Soup

You can easily make this soup ahead, then simply return it to the slow cooker and heat through for an hour on High until piping hot but not bubbling.

 5–6 hours, plus overnight soaking   8   easily halved

- 1kg/2lb 4oz ham hock
- 200g/7oz split peas, soaked overnight
- 2 onions, roughly chopped
- 2 carrots, roughly chopped
- 2 bay leaves
- 1 celery stick, roughly chopped
- 300g/10oz frozen peas
- crusty bread and butter, to serve

1 Put the ham in a very large pan with 2 litres/3½ pints water and bring to the boil. Remove from the heat and drain off the water.

2 Heat the slow cooker if necessary. Add the ham to the pot with the split peas, onion, carrots, bay and celery. Cover with the lid and cook on High for 4–5 hours until the ham is tender enough to shred – check occasionally as the ham cooks and softens. You can halve it if you want, so it is all submerged under the liquid.

3 When it is ready, lift out the ham and bay leaves, and tip the frozen peas into the slow cooker. Cook for another 30 mins while you prepare the ham. Peel off and discard the skin, and while it is still hot (wear a clean pair of rubber gloves), shred the meat. Blend the soup until smooth, adding a splash of water if too thick, and then mix in most of the ham. Serve in bowls with the remaining ham scattered on top, and eat with crusty bread and butter.

PER SERVING 292 kcals, fat 11 g, saturates 4g, carbs 23g, sugars 5g, fibre 5g, protein 26g, salt 3.5g

Thai Chicken Soup

This is perfect for a Monday night if you have a chicken carcass from your Sunday roast. Any leftover meat can be shredded and added with the noodles and veg.

 7–8 hours 4

- 140g/5oz soba or wholewheat noodles
- 100g/4oz beansprouts
- 2 pak choi, leaves separated
- 1 red chilli, deseeded and sliced
- 1 tbsp soy sauce
- 2 tbsp honey
- juice 1 lime, plus extra wedges to squeeze over
- 4 spring onions, sliced, to garnish
- ½ small bunch mint, roughly chopped, to garnish

FOR THE BROTH
- 1 roasted chicken carcass
- thumb-sized piece ginger, bashed and sliced
- 1 garlic clove, crushed
- 2 spring onions, sliced
- 5 peppercorns

1 To make the broth, heat the slow cooker if necessary. Put the chicken carcass in the slow cooker pot. Just cover it with hot water, then add the rest of the broth ingredients, and cover and cook on Low for 6–7 hours.
2 Strain the chicken broth into a clean pan. Carefully pick out any pieces of chicken and return them to the broth, but discard the bones. Put the broth back in the slow cooker pot.
3 Add the noodles, beansprouts, pak choi, red chilli, soy sauce, honey and lime juice, adding the squeezed lime halves to the pot, too. Cook on High, covered, for 30 mins more.
4 Ladle the soup into bowls, scatter over the spring onions and mint leaves, and serve with the lime wedges for squeezing over.

PER SERVING 206 kcals, fat 2g, saturates none, carbs 35g, sugars 7g, fibre 2g, protein 15g, salt 1.9g

Courgette, Potato & Cheddar Soup

This makes a big batch – perfect for using up a glut of cheap courgettes and potatoes, but if your slow cooker is small, simply halve the quantities of the ingredients.

 4 hours 8 easily halved

- 500g/1lb 2oz potatoes, unpeeled and roughly chopped
- 2 vegetable stock cubes
- 1kg/2lb 4oz courgettes, roughly chopped
- bunch spring onions, sliced, save 1 onion, thinly sliced, to garnish
- 100g/4oz extra mature cheddar or vegetarian alternative, grated, plus a little extra to garnish
- good grating fresh nutmeg

1 Heat the slow cooker if necessary. Put the potatoes in the slow cooker pot with just enough water to cover them and crumble in the stock cubes. Cover and cook for 3 hours on High until the potatoes are tender.

2 Scoop out a couple of ladlefuls of stock and save for the end. Add the courgettes and spring onions, put the lid back on and cook for 30 mins more until the courgettes are tender.

3 Take off the heat, then stir in the cheese and season with the nutmeg, salt and some black pepper. Whizz to a thick soup with a stick blender, adding the reserved stock until you get the consistency you like. Serve scattered with the extra grated cheddar, spring onions and black pepper. Or cool and freeze in freezer bags or containers with good lids for up to 3 months.

PER SERVING 131 kcals, fat 6g, saturates 3g, carbs 14g, sugars 3g, fibre 2g, protein 7g, salt 1.3g

Hot & Sour Broth with Prawns

This makes a great starter before a Chinese meal; it's simple, but the key is allowing time to flavour the broth.

 1½ hours, or up to a day if you like   4

- 3 tbsp rice vinegar or white wine vinegar
- 500ml/18fl oz chicken stock
- 1 tbsp soy sauce
- 1–2 tbsp golden caster sugar
- thumb-sized piece ginger, peeled and thinly sliced
- 1 lemongrass stalk, outer woody leaves removed and finely sliced
- 2 small hot red chillies, thinly sliced
- 3 spring onions, thinly sliced
- 300g/10oz small raw peeled prawns, from a sustainable source

1 Heat the slow cooker if necessary. Put the vinegar, stock, soy sauce, sugar (start with 1 tablespoon and add the second at the end if you want the soup sweeter), ginger, lemongrass and chillies in the slow cooker pot. Cover and cook on High for 1 hour, or on Low for 4–8 hours, if you have time.

2 When you're nearly ready to serve, add the spring onions and prawns. Cover and cook on High for 20–30 mins until the prawns are just cooked.

PER SERVING 93 kcals, fat 1g, saturates none, carbs 5g, sugars 5g, fibre none, protein 17g, salt 1.39g

Parsnip Soup with Parsley Cream

This gorgeous soup makes a great starter at a winter dinner party, with the extra special touch of crispy fried-parsnip croutons and silky parsley cream.

 4-9 hours   6

- 1 onion, finely chopped
- 1 tbsp olive oil
- 700g/1lb 9oz parsnips, cut into chunks
- 3 bay leaves
- 300ml/½ pint whole milk, plus a drop more if necessary
- 300ml/½ pint vegetable stock

FOR THE PARSLEY PUREÉ & CREAM
- 2 x 80g packs curly parsley
- 150ml/¼ pint double cream
- 150ml/¼ pint whipping cream, whipped to soft peaks for the garnish
- 1 parsnip, cut into small cubes
- 1 tbsp olive oil

1 Heat the slow cooker if necessary. Soften the onion in the oil in a frying pan for 10 mins until softened. Transfer to the pot with the parsnips, bay leaves, milk and stock. Cover and cook on Low for 6–8 hours or on High for 3–4 hours until the parsnips are tender.

2 Remove the bay leaves and drain the parsnips, reserving the liquid. Whizz the parsnips in a blender, adding a little reserved liquid at a time until a good soup consistency.

3 For the parsley purée, blanch the parsley in boiling water for 30 seconds, then refresh in iced water. Squeeze out any water, then whizz in a blender with the double cream until smooth. Fold a little of the purée through the whipped cream. Season and chill.

4 For the garnish, fry the parsnip cubes in the oil until golden and tender.

5 Reheat the soup. Put the purée into six bowls, top with the soup, then the parsley cream and the parsnip cubes.

PER SERVING 393 kcals, fat 30g, saturates 15g, carbs 25g, sugars 15g, fibre 8g, protein 7g, salt 0.32g

Pea & Watercress Soup

A perfect summer soup that you can adapt so you can serve it all year round. Use spring onions, rocket and sorrel in spring; frozen peas and leeks in winter.

 3½ hours   4

- 1 tbsp olive oil
- 1 onion, finely chopped
- 1 garlic clove, roughly chopped
- 1 medium potato, cut into small chunks
- 700ml/1¼ pints vegetable stock
- 300g/10oz fresh peas (or frozen if out of season)
- 100g/4oz watercress
- leaves from 2 mint sprigs, plus extra, chopped, to garnish
- 100ml/3½fl oz double cream
- crusty bread, to serve

1 Heat the slow cooker if necessary. Heat the oil in a frying pan, then gently fry the onion and garlic for 5 mins or until soft. Scrape into the slow cooker pot with the potato and stock. Cover and cook on High for 2½ hours until the potato is almost cooked.

2 Scatter in the peas and watercress, stir, cover, then cook for 20–30 mins more until everything is tender. Add the mint leaves and blitz with a stick blender until smooth. Stir in the cream and season to taste. Serve ladled into bowls, scattered with more mint and some cracked black pepper. Serve with crusty bread.

PER SERVING 256 kcals, fat 18g, saturates 8g, carbs 17g, sugars 5g, fibre 5g, protein 8g, salt 0.21g

Curried Lentil, Parsnip & Apple Soup

If you have a small slow cooker, simply halve the ingredients.

 3½ hours   6-8   easily halved

- 1-2 tbsp sunflower oil
- 3 tbsp Madras curry paste
- 2 medium onions, roughly chopped
- 500g/1lb 2oz parsnips, peeled and cut into chunks
- 140g/5oz red lentils
- 2 Bramley apples (about 400g/14oz), peeled, cored and cut into chunks
- 1 litre/1¾ pints vegetable or chicken stock, made with 1 stock cube
- natural yogurt and coriander leaves, to serve (optional)

1 Heat the slow cooker if necessary. Heat the oil in a large saucepan and fry the curry paste and onions together over a medium heat for 3 mins, stirring. Add the parsnips, lentils and apple. Pour over the stock and bring to a simmer.

2 Tip into the slow cooker, cover and cook on Low for 3 hours until the vegetables are tender.

3 Blitz with a stick blender until smooth. (Or leave to cool for a few mins, then blend in a food processor.) Adjust the seasoning to taste, and if it is a little thick dilute with boiling water to your desired consistency. Serve with yogurt and garnish with fresh coriander, if you like.

PER SERVING (8) 204 kcals, fat 5g, saturates 1g, carbs 24g, sugars 10g, fibre 8g, protein 12g, salt 0.7g

Carrot & Coriander Soup

Everyone loves this soup and it's simplicity itself to make with just a few low-cost ingredients. Put on to cook first thing, ready for a light lunch.

 3½ hours   4    easily doubled

- 1 tbsp vegetable oil
- 1 onion, chopped
- 1 tsp ground coriander
- 1 large potato, chopped
- 450g/1lb carrots, peeled and chopped
- 1 litre/1¾ pints vegetable or chicken stock
- handful fresh coriander (about ½ a pack), plus a few sprigs to garnish

1 Heat the slow cooker if necessary. Heat the oil in a large pan, add the onion, then fry for 5 mins until softened. Stir in the ground coriander and cook for 1 min. Add the potato, carrots and stock and bring to the boil.

2 Tip into the slow cooker then cook on Low for 3 hours until the carrots are tender.

3 Add the coriander and seasoning then blitz with a stick blender until smooth. (Or use a food processor – you may need to do this in two batches). Serve topped with the remaining coriander if you like.

PER SERVING 115 kcals, fat 4g, saturates 1g, carbs 19g, sugars 12g, fibre 5g, protein 3g, salt 0.46g

Walkers' Wild Mushroom, Bacon & Barley Broth

Dried porcini mushrooms give this soup a rich flavour, which the barley and veg soaks up. Do try it with a sprinkling of cheese – it lifts a bowl of soup into a meal in itself.

 7½ hours   6

- 200g pack lardons, or rashers bacon, cut into small pieces
- 2 onions, chopped
- 2 garlic cloves, crushed
- 1 glass dry white wine
- 30g pack dried porcini or dried mixed wild mushrooms
- 4 medium carrots, chopped into small pieces
- 3 celery sticks, thinly sliced
- 1 sprig each rosemary and thyme
- 1 litre/1¾ pints chicken stock
- 100g/4oz pearl barley, well rinsed
- ½ small head spring greens or chunk of Savoy cabbage, finely shredded
- Small wedge Parmesan or any strong hard cheese, grated, to sprinkle
- crusty bread, to serve

1 Sizzle the bacon for 10 mins until golden. Add the onion and garlic, lower the heat and soften for 5 mins. Tip in the wine, increase the heat and bring to a simmer.

2 Meanwhile, put the mushrooms into a jug and fill up to the 400ml/14fl oz mark with boiling water. Soak for 10 mins.

3 Heat the slow cooker if necessary. Scrape the bacon mixture into the pot. Lift the mushrooms out of their juice with a slotted spoon and roughly chop. Add to the pot with the carrots, celery and herbs. Pour over the stock, plus the mushroom soaking liquid – avoiding the last few drops as they can be gritty. Cover and cook on Low for 5 hours. Add the barley and cook on Low for 1 hour.

4 Add the greens or cabbage, and cook for 30 mins on High (if the cabbage doesn't fit, boil it separately then stir in to serve). Season, then serve with cheese sprinkled over the top and crusty bread.

PER SERVING 264 kcals, fat 9g, saturates 3g, carbs 26g, sugars 9g, fibre 5g, protein 13g, salt 1.6g

Broccoli Soup with Goat's Cheese Croutons

This soup is smart enough to serve as a starter at a fancy dinner party, or if you prefer something more substantial for lunch, swap the croutons for a blue-cheese toastie.

 3½ hours 4

- 1 onion, finely diced
- 1 tsp olive oil or knob butter
- 1 medium potato, finely diced
- 700ml/1¼ pints vegetable stock
- 400g/14oz broccoli, head broken into florets and stalk thinly sliced
- 100g/4oz rocket leaves
- 8 thin slices baguette
- 150g pack soft goat's cheese

1 Fry the onion gently in the olive oil or butter for 5–10 mins, until soft.
2 Heat the slow cooker if necessary. Tip in the softened onions, then add the potato, vegetable stock and plenty of seasoning. Cover and cook on High for 1 hour, then add the broccoli and cover and cook for 2 hours more until the potato and broccoli are tender.
3 Stir in the rocket, cover and set aside for 10 mins, then whizz the soup in a food processor, or use a stick blender, until smooth. Return to the pot and keep warm.
4 Toast the baguette slices, spread each with a little goat's cheese, then grill if you like, or serve as they are with the soup.

PER SERVING 287 kcals, fat 12g, saturates 7g, carbs 27g, sugars 7g, fibre 6g, protein 16g, salt 1.3g

Creamy Tomato Soup

This soup can be made all year round as it uses only canned tomatoes and passata. Make this for Bonfire Night and serve with plenty of cheesy bread rolls on the side.

 3½ hours   6

- 1½ tbsp olive oil
- 1 onion, chopped
- 1 celery stick, chopped
- 140g/5oz carrots, chopped
- 250g/9oz potatoes, diced
- 2 bay leaves
- 2½ tbsp tomato purée
- 1 tbsp golden caster sugar, plus extra to taste
- 1 tbsp red or white wine vinegar
- 2 x 400g cans chopped tomatoes
- 250g/9oz passata
- 1 vegetable stock cube
- 200ml/7fl oz full-fat milk

1 Heat the slow cooker if necessary. Put the oil and onion in a frying pan, and cook gently for 10–15 mins until the onion is softened. Boil the kettle.

2 Scrape the onion into the slow cooker pot with the celery, carrots, potatoes, bay leaves, tomato purée, sugar, vinegar, chopped tomatoes and passata. Crumble in the stock cube. Add 300ml/½ pint boiling water. Cover and cook on High for 3 hours until the potato is tender, then remove the bay leaves.

3 Purée the soup with a stick blender (or ladle into a food processor in batches) until very smooth. Season to taste and add a pinch more sugar if it needs it. The soup can now be cooled and chilled for up to 2 days, or frozen for up to 3 months.

4 To serve, reheat the soup, stirring in the milk until hot – try not to let it boil.

PER SERVING 148 kcals, fat 5g, saturates 1g, carbs 21g, sugars 14g, fibre 4g, protein 5g, salt 0.9g

Herby Pressed Ham with Spiced Apple Compote

This starter takes a little effort, but makes an impressive restaurant-quality starter if you love to entertain. You could also serve with a bought chutney.

7 hours, plus cooling and chilling 4

- 25g/1oz butter
- 1 shop-bought malt loaf (about 250g/9oz), cut into bite-sized pieces

FOR THE HAM
- 1kg/2lb 4oz ham hocks
- 1 onion, quartered
- 2 bay leaves
- 1 cinnamon stick
- ½ tsp black peppercorns
- 3 gelatine leaves
- 3 tbsp chopped flat-leaf parsley
- 2 tbsp chopped tarragon

FOR THE APPLE COMPOTE
- 400g/14oz Bramley apples, peeled, cored and diced
- 25g/1oz butter
- 1 cinnamon stick
- 1 star anise
- 4 cloves
- 2 tbsp light brown sugar

FOR THE VINAIGRETTE
- 1 tbsp chopped tarragon
- 1 tbsp cider vinegar
- 2 tbsp olive oil

1 To make the ham, heat the slow cooker if necessary. Put the ham hocks in the slow cooker pot with the onion, bay leaves, cinnamon stick and peppercorns. Cover with water, cover the pot, and cook on Low for 6 hours until the hocks are really tender. Cool.

2 Put the gelatine in a bowl of cold water to soften for around 5 mins, then drain. Strain 300ml/½ pint of the ham cooking liquid through a fine sieve and pour it into a pan. Heat until just simmering then remove from the heat and add the gelatine. Stir well and leave to cool.

3 Strip the ham from the bones and chop into small pieces. Line four x 200ml ramekins with cling film and add a third of the cooked ham to each to form the base layer. Pour over a little of the gelatine liquid, then sprinkle in a layer of parsley. Next, add another third of the ham and some more gelatine liquid. The next layer should be the tarragon, followed by the remaining ham and the rest of the gelatine liquid. Once all the layers are complete, cover the surface of each with cling film, then a layer of foil and chill with some weights on top for at least 2 hours.

4 For the apple compote, Put the apples in a pan with the butter, 4 tablespoons water and the spices. Cook gently until softened. Remove the cinnamon stick, star anise and cloves, and stir in the sugar. Heat gently until the sugar has dissolved then cool.

5 To make the vinaigrette, whisk the tarragon with the vinegar and oil, then season to taste.

6 Put the 25g butter in a non-stick frying pan and heat until foaming. Drop in the cubes of malt loaf and fry for around 2 mins, turning regularly, to lightly brown them on all sides.

7 To serve, turn out a ramekin onto each plate and carefully remove the cling film. Add spoonfuls of the apple compote and the cubes of toasted malt loaf. Drizzle a little of the vinaigrette over the plate and ham then serve.

PER SERVING 568 kcals, fat 26g, saturates 10g, carbs 45g, sugars 16g, fibre 3g, protein 36g, salt 1.3g

Country Terrine with Black Pepper & Thyme

This may seem an unusual dish to cook in a slow cooker, but it's a brilliant way to stop the meat drying out.

🕐 4–5 hours, plus overnight chilling   🥧 8

- butter, for greasing
- 750g/1lb 10oz rashers pork belly
- 1 tbsp dried thyme
- 1 tsp black peppercorns
- 2 x 225g tubs frozen chicken livers, thawed
- 4 tbsp red or white wine (optional)
- 5 rashers smoked streaky bacon
- cocktail gherkins or chutney, and toast or bread, to serve

1 Heat the slow cooker if necessary. Butter a 1kg loaf tin. Finely chop three of the pork belly rashers and mix with the thyme and peppercorns. Set aside. Put the remaining pork belly into a food processor with two-thirds of the chicken livers, the wine (if using) and 1 teaspoon salt, then blend to make a smooth pâté.

2 Spoon half the pâté into the loaf tin, then top with the chopped pork mixture and remaining livers. Spoon over the rest of the pâté, then lay the bacon on top.

3 Cover the tin with foil and put in the slow cooker. Pour enough boiling water into the cooker pot to come halfway up the sides of the loaf tin. Cover and bake on High for 3–4 hours until firm and the juices come clear when poked with a skewer. Drain off any liquid left in the tin.

4 Cool, then put another loaf tin on top and weight it down with cans to compress it. Leave overnight in the fridge before slicing. Serve with the gherkins or chutney and toast or crusty bread.

PER SERVING 330 kcals, fat 23g, saturates 9g, carbs none, sugars none, fibre none, protein 30g, salt 0.64g

Chinese Roast Duck with Pancakes

Cooking Chinese food doesn't have to be complicated when you've got a slow cooker, so let it do the hard work for you and simply finish the duck quickly under the grill.

 5–6 hours 4

- 1 oven-ready duck
- 2 tsp Chinese five-spice powder
- 2 star anise
- 1 orange, peel cut off in strips, fruit halved
- 2 tbsp Chinese black vinegar (optional)
- 75ml/2½fl oz Shaohsing rice wine or dry Sherry
- 100ml/3½fl oz chicken stock
- 30 Chinese pancakes
- 6 spring onions, cut into finger lengths and shredded, ½ cucumber, cut into matchsticks, and hoisin sauce, to serve

1 Heat the slow cooker if necessary. Loosen the skin on the duck by wriggling first your fingers and then your hand between it and the flesh until it pulls away – be careful not to break the skin. Trim off any excess fat from the cavity and skin around the neck. Rub the skin all over with the five spice plus a good sprinkling of salt. Push the star anise, orange peel and orange halves inside the cavity and put the duck in the slow cooker.

2 Spoon over the vinegar, if using, rice wine or Sherry and stock. Cover and cook on High for 4–5 hours until very tender. When cooked, flash the duck under a hot grill to crisp up the skin. Let it rest for 10 mins then shred the meat and skin – you may need to wear gloves to do this as it will be very hot. Heat the pancakes and serve the duck with all of the accompaniments.

PER SERVING 705 kcals, fat 46g, saturates 12g, carbs 42g, sugars 5g, fibre 3g, protein 30g, salt 1.08g

Pesto & Mozzarella-stuffed Mushrooms

Italian green basil and pine-nut pesto and creamy mascarpone make a good base for these stuffed mushrooms, ideal as a starter for four, or a light veggie lunch for two.

 3½ hours 2-4

- 2 tbsp olive oil, plus extra for greasing
- 1 onion, chopped
- 4 large Portobello mushrooms, stalks finely chopped
- 100g/4oz light mascarpone
- zest and juice ½ lemon
- 4 tbsp basil pesto
- 125g ball light mozzarella, chopped
- 25g/1oz dried breadcrumbs
- large handful rocket leaves
- 100g/4oz cherry tomatoes, halved

1 Heat half the oil in a small pan and cook the onion and chopped mushroom stalks for 5–8 mins until soft. Tip into a bowl, allow to cool slightly, then add the mascarpone, lemon zest, pesto, mozzarella and seasoning.

2 Heat the slow cooker to High. Grease the inside of the slow cooker with a little oil and add the whole mushrooms, in a single layer. Divide the stuffing among the mushrooms, spreading to fill the middle of each one. Top each with breadcrumbs and a grind of black pepper, then cover with the lid and cook for 3 hours until the mushrooms are tender. If you want to crisp the tops, heat grill to high, slide the mushrooms on to a baking sheet and cook for a few mins, until golden.

3 Meanwhile, make the dressing. Whisk the remaining oil with the lemon juice and some seasoning. Dress the rocket leaves and tomatoes and serve with the mushrooms.

PER SERVING (4) 280 kcals, fat 19g, saturates 6g, carbs 24g, sugars 6g, fibre 3g, protein 15g, salt 0.9g

Spinach-baked Eggs with Parmesan & Tomato Toasts

Baked eggs are simple to do and make a really good summery starter or light lunch for friends. This version is served with delicious tomatoey toasts.

 1½ hours 4

- 85g/3oz softened butter
- 3 tbsp grated Parmesan
- 6 shredded basil leaves
- 1 tbsp finely chopped sundried tomatoes
- 400g/14oz spinach leaves
- 4 eggs
- 8–12 slices French bread

1 Mash together the butter, Parmesan, basil and sundried tomatoes, and chill.
2 Wash the spinach and trim off any thick stalks. Put into a large pan, then cook, covered, for about 2–3 mins or until the spinach is wilted. Drain well, pressing out all the excess water, then return to the pan with about a quarter of the butter mix, stirring until the spinach is glistening.
3 Heat the slow cooker if necessary. Divide the spinach among four buttered ramekins, then break an egg into each. Season with salt and black pepper, then top with a slice of the butter mix. Sit in the base of a slow cooker, then pour in boiling water around the ramekins until half full. Cover and cook for 30–45 mins on Low, until the eggs are to your liking.
4 Meanwhile, grill the bread on one side until crisp, then spread the other side with the remaining butter and grill until crisp. Serve the eggs with the toast on the side.

PER SERVING 494 kcals, fat 33g, saturates 18g, carbs 31g, sugars 4g, fibre 4g, protein 20g, salt 2.23g

Pea Risotto

This risotto makes the most of peas by incorporating pea purée and pea shoots, as well as little sweet peas. This serves six as a starter, four as a main course.

 1½ hours   4-6

- 50g/2oz butter
- 1 onion, finely chopped
- 300g/10oz frozen or cooked fresh peas
- 1 litre/1¾ pints hot vegetable stock
- 350g/12oz risotto rice, rinsed until water runs clear
- 25g/1oz Parmesan or vegetarian alternative, grated
- 2 good handfuls pea shoots, to garnish
- extra virgin olive oil, to drizzle (optional)

1 Heat the slow cooker if necessary. Melt the butter in a frying pan, add the onion and gently soften for about 10 mins until really soft. Meanwhile, put 100g/4oz of the peas into a food processor with a ladleful of stock and whizz until completely puréed.

2 Put the onion into the slow cooker pot and stir in the rice and remaining stock. Cover and cook on High for 1 hour or until the rice is just tender and creamy.

3 Stir in the puréed peas, remaining whole peas, Parmesan or vegetarian alternative and some seasoning, then turn off the heat, re-cover and leave to stand for a few mins. Give the risotto a final stir, spoon into shallow bowls and top with some pea shoots and a drizzle of olive oil, if you like.

PER SERVING (4) 503 kcals, fat 14g, saturates 8g, carbs 80g, sugars 6g, fibre 8g, protein 14g, salt 1g

Easy Cheese Fondue

Using mild cheese in this recipe means everyone can enjoy it, but if you fancy just making this for grown ups you can swap the Cheddar for something with more bite.

 1½ hours   6-8

- 2 tbsp cider vinegar
- 1 tsp cornflour
- 3 tbsp crème fraîche
- 250g/9oz cheddar, grated
- 250g/9oz Gruyère, grated

SUGGESTIONS FOR DIPPING
- 4 thick slices bread, toasted in chunks
- 2 carrots, cut into batons
- 2 peppers, deseeded and cut into strips
- 2 celery sticks, thickly sliced
- 200g/7oz mini salamis or 1 thin salami, cut into bite-sized chunks

1 Heat the slow cooker if necessary. Mix the vinegar with the cornflour, then stir in the crème fraîche. Scatter the cheeses into the slow cooker pot then dot the crème fraîche mixture on top. Cover and cook on High for 1 hour, stirring halfway, until the cheeses have melted.

2 Season with pepper and give the fondue a good whisk. Then serve with your favourites for dipping in.

PER SERVING (8) 374 kcals, fat 31g, saturates 20g, carbs 1g, sugars none, fibre none, protein 22g, salt 1.48g

Spaghetti alle Vongole

Clams are easy to cook with – they just need a little preparation first.

🕐 2–2½ hours   🥧 2-3   🌓 easily doubled

- 500g/1lb 2oz fresh clams in shells
- 2 ripe tomatoes, chopped
- 2 tbsp olive oil
- 1 fat garlic clove, chopped
- 1 small or ½ a large fresh red chilli, finely chopped
- splash white wine (about ½ small glass)
- 140g/5oz spaghetti
- 2 tbsp chopped parsley

1 Heat the slow cooker if necessary. Rinse the clams in several changes of cold water. Discard any that are open or damaged. Add to the slow cooker pot with the chopped tomatoes, olive oil, garlic, chilli and white wine. Cook on High for 1½–2 hours, until the clams are open.
2 Meanwhile, cook the spaghetti according to the pack instructions. Drain the pasta, then tip the pasta into the slow cooker with the parsley and toss together. Serve in bowls with bread for mopping up the juices.

PER SERVING (2) 409 kcals, fat 13g, saturates 2g, carbs 56g, sugars 5g, fibre 3g, protein 16g, salt 0.10g

Creamy Spiced Mussels

If you have never bought fresh mussels before, you'll find they are surprisingly quick and easy to prepare.

 3 hours   4

- 2 shallots, finely chopped
- 25g/1oz butter
- 1 tsp plain flour
- 1–2 tsp curry paste
- 150ml/¼ pint dry white wine
- 2kg/4lb 8oz fresh mussels
- 100ml/3½fl oz crème fraîche
- chopped parsley, to garnish

1 Heat the slow cooker if necessary. Put the shallots, butter, flour, curry paste and wine into the slow cooker pot. Cover and cook on High for 1 hour.

2 Scrub the mussels in a large bowl of cold water and discard any that are open. Tip into the slow cooker pot, re-cover and cook on High for 1½ hours until just about all the mussels open and are cooked. Discard any that haven't opened during cooking.

3 Stir the crème fraîche into the sauce, warming it through. Divide the mussels among four bowls and pour over the sauce. Scatter with parsley and serve with bread to mop up the juices or chips if you fancy these for a main meal.

PER SERVING 285 kcals, fat 18g, saturates 10g, carbs 6g, sugars none, fibre 1g, protein 19g, salt 1.27g

Chapter 2:

FAMILY FAVOURITES

. . . .

Honey Crunch Granola

This might seem an unusual dish to make in the slow cooker but it really works – see for yourself!

🕐 2 hours, plus cooling   ⏰ Makes 1kg/2¼lb

- 125ml/4fl oz sunflower oil
- 100ml/3½fl oz malt extract
- 100ml/3½fl oz clear honey
- 250g/9oz rolled oats
- 250g/9oz jumbo oats
- 25g/1oz desiccated coconut
- 50g/2oz sunflower seeds
- 25g/1oz sesame seeds
- 140g/5oz whole brazil nuts
- 100g/4oz mixed dried fruit (such as sultanas, chopped apricots or dates)

1 Heat the slow cooker if necessary. Put in the oil, malt extract and honey, and cook on High for 30 mins, without a cover, until the malt extract becomes runny. Stir, then add in the remaining ingredients, except the brazil nuts and dried fruit, and stir until evenly coated.

2 Turn the cooker to Low and cook, covered, for 45 mins, then remove the lid, stir, and cook for 30 mins more until crisp. Tip out on to a baking tin, or into a bowl, to cool and stir in the brazil nuts and fruit. Once cool, transfer to a jar or other airtight container and keep for up to a month.

PER SERVING 591 kcals, fat 34g, saturates 7g, carbs 63g, sugars 24g, fibre 6g, protein 12g, salt 0.04g

Spiced Coconut Porridge with Cranberry & Orange Compote

When it's chilly, it's got to be porridge. Put this on first thing while you get ready, then sit down to breakfast with the family. The compote can be made the night before if you like.

 2 hours  4

- 175g/6oz porridge oats
- 400ml can coconut milk
- 3 tbsp soft light brown sugar
- 1 tsp ground cinnamon
- good grating of nutmeg, plus extra to serve
- 160ml can coconut cream, plus shaved toasted coconut, to serve (optional)

FOR THE COMPOTE
- 3 tbsp light brown soft sugar
- 3 oranges, peeled and sliced
- 250g/9oz fresh or frozen cranberries

1 Heat the slow cooker if necessary. Mix together the oats, 700ml/1¼ pints water, the coconut milk, sugar, spices and a pinch of salt in the pot and stir well. Cover and cook on High for 1½ hours, until it's thick and creamy. Add a splash of milk or water if you like it thinner.

2 Meanwhile, prepare the compote. Put the sugar and 2 tablespoons water in a frying pan and heat to dissolve the sugar. Once bubbling, add the oranges and cranberries. Stir, then turn up the heat and leave to bubble for a few mins until most of the liquid evaporates and the compote becomes thick and sticky.

3 To serve, spoon the porridge into bowls, top with the cranberry & orange compote, a swirl of coconut cream, some shaved coconut and an extra grating of nutmeg, if you like.

PER SERVING 469 kcals, fat 13g, saturates 8g, carbs 73g, sugars 47g, fibre 7g, protein 17g, salt 0.3g

Apple & Spice Tea Loaf

This loaf looks as good as anything you might pick up at a cake shop or farmers' market, and tastes spicy, fruity and light.

 2½–3½ hours  Cuts into 10 slices

- 175g/6oz butter, plus extra for greasing
- 175g/6oz light muscovado sugar, plus 1 tsp
- 3 eggs, beaten
- 1 eating apple, peeled and cored
- 1 tsp vanilla extract
- 200g/7oz dried mixed vine fruits
- 85g/3oz ground almonds
- 1 tsp each baking powder and ground cinnamon
- 175g/6oz plain flour
- ½ tsp ground nutmeg
- splash lemon or orange juice
- 1 tbsp marmalade or apricot jam

1 Heat the slow cooker if necessary, with an upturned saucer in the bottom. Butter a 900g loaf tin and line with baking paper, or use a liner. Beat together the butter and sugar until pale, then beat in the eggs one by one. Grate half the apple and mix in with the vanilla, dried fruit and almonds. Mix the baking powder, flour and spices together with a pinch of salt, then fold into the mix until even. Spoon into the tin and level the top.

2 Thinly slice the remaining apple half, toss with the lemon or orange juice, poke the slices a little way into the batter, then sprinkle with the extra teaspoon of sugar. Put in the slow cooker, cover with the lid, and bake on High for 2–3 hours until a skewer poked into the centre comes out clean. Cool in the tin.

3 To finish the cake, melt the marmalade or jam in a small pan, then brush it over the cake to glaze the top. Serve in slices, spread with a little butter.

PER SLICE 416 kcals, fat 22g, saturates 10g, carbs 50g, sugars 36g, fibre 2g, protein 7g, salt 0.54g

Big-batch Bolognese

Don't worry if your slow cooker is too small for this recipe, it is really easy to reduce the quantities, and it will taste delicious no matter how much you make.

🕐 7½–9½ hours　　◔ 12　　◑ easily halved

- 4 tbsp olive oil
- 6 rashers smoked bacon, chopped
- 1.5kg/3lb 5oz lean minced beef
- 4 onions, finely chopped
- 3 carrots, finely chopped
- 4 celery sticks, finely chopped
- 500g/1lb 2oz mushrooms, sliced
- 8 garlic cloves, crushed
- 2 tbsp dried mixed herbs
- 2 bay leaves
- 4 x 400g cans chopped tomatoes
- 6 tbsp tomato purée
- large glass red wine (optional)
- 4 tbsp red wine vinegar
- 1 tbsp caster sugar
- pasta, to serve
- Parmesan shavings, to garnish

1 Heat the slow cooker if necessary. Heat the oil in a very large pan and fry the bacon and mince, in batches, until browned. Tip into the slow cooker and stir in the vegetables, garlic, herbs, chopped tomatoes, purée, wine, if using, vinegar and sugar with some seasoning.
2 Cover and cook on Low for 6–8 hours, then uncover, turn to High and cook for another hour until thick and saucy, and the mince is tender. Serve with pasta and scattered shavings of Parmesan.

PER SERVING 321 kcals, fat 19g, saturates 7g, carbs 8g, sugars 7g, fibre 2g, protein 31g, salt 1.27g

Cottage Pie

· ·

This makes enough to feed an army, but it freezes really well and can also be halved very easily if you have a small slow cooker.

🕐 5–6 hours   🥧 10   ◑ easily halved

- 3 tbsp olive oil
- 1.25kg/2lb 12oz minced beef
- 2 onions, finely chopped
- 3 carrots, chopped
- 3 celery sticks, chopped
- 3 tbsp plain flour
- 1 tbsp tomato purée
- large glass red wine (optional)
- 500ml/18fl oz beef stock
- 4 tbsp Worcestershire sauce
- few thyme sprigs
- 2 bay leaves

FOR THE MASH
- 1.8kg/4lb potatoes, chopped
- 225ml/8fl oz milk
- 25g/1oz butter
- 200g/7oz strong cheddar, grated

1 Heat the slow cooker if necessary. Heat the oil in a large pan and fry the mince until browned in batches. Tip into the slow cooker pot and stir in the vegetables, flour, purée, wine (if using), stock, Worcestershire sauce and herbs with some seasoning. Cover and cook on High for 4–5 hours.

2 Make the mash. Boil the potatoes until tender, then mash with the milk, butter and three-quarters of the cheese. Season.

3 Spoon the beef mixture into ovenproof dishes. Pipe or spoon on the mash, then sprinkle over the remaining cheese. Grill until golden.

· ·

PER SERVING 600 kcals, fat 34g, saturates 16g, carbs 40g, sugars 7g, fibre 4g, protein 37g, salt 1.15g

Chilli con Carne

This is an ideal dish for entertaining families with kids, and any leftovers freeze really well; so if you've got a very big slow cooker it's definitely worth making a double batch.

🕐 8½–10½ hours   🥧 4-6   ◑ easily halved or doubled

- 2 tbsp olive oil
- 2 large onions, halved and sliced
- 3 large garlic cloves, chopped
- 2 tbsp mild chilli powder
- 2 tsp each ground cumin and dried oregano
- 1kg/2lb 4oz lean minced beef
- 400g can chopped tomatoes
- 2 large red peppers, deseeded and cut into chunks
- 10 sundried tomatoes, halved
- 3 x 400g cans red kidney beans, drained and rinsed
- 2 beef stock cubes
- avocado, salad, rice or tortilla chips and some soured cream, to serve

1 Heat the slow cooker if necessary. Heat the oil in a large pan and fry the onions for 8 mins. Add the garlic, spices and oregano, and cook for 1 min, then gradually add the mince, stirring well until browned. Tip into the slow cooker pot and stir in the chopped tomatoes, peppers, sundried tomatoes and beans, then crumble in the stock cubes and season to taste.

2 Cover and cook on Low for 8–10 hours. Serve with avocado or a big salad with avocado in it, some rice or tortilla chips and a bowl of soured cream.

PER SERVING (4) 820 kcals, fat 34g, saturates 12g, carbs 58g, sugars 21g, fibre 16g, protein 75g, salt 3.5g

Turkey Pasta Bake

Here's a great family dish teenagers will love. Pop the mince in the slow cooker to gently simmer for a few hours then top with the pasta and bake.

 4 hours   4-6

- 1 tbsp olive oil
- 2 onions, finely chopped
- 500g/1lb 2oz turkey thigh mince
- 2 garlic cloves, crushed
- 2 x 400g cans chopped tomatoes
- 1 tbsp chipotle paste or bbq sauce
- 1 chicken stock cube
- 400g/14oz large pasta shells

FOR THE TOPPING
- 250g tub mascarpone
- 200g/7oz cheddar, grated
- 2 tbsp grated Parmesan

1 Heat the slow cooker if necessary. Heat the olive oil in a large pan and fry the onions for 8-10 mins until softened. Add the mince and brown all over. Once browned, add the garlic, tomatoes, chipotle paste or bbq sauce and chicken stock cube, and bring to the boil. Tip into the slow cooker and cook on Low for 3 hours. Season to taste.

2 When the mince is nearly ready, boil the pasta following pack instructions, then drain, reserving some of the water. Warm through the mascarpone with a splash of the hot pasta water over a low heat. Add 140g/5oz cheddar, season and stir to combine.

3 Heat oven to 200C/180C fan/gas 6. Transfer the turkey to a large baking dish. Stir the cheese sauce through the pasta and pour over the mince. Sprinkle the remaining cheddar and the Parmesan on top. Bake in the oven for 20 mins or until golden and crisping at the edges.

PER SERVING (6) 647 kcals, fat 33g, saturates 20g, carbs 44g, sugars 9g, fibre 2g, protein 41g, salt 1.1g

Meatball Stroganoff

Serve these meatballs with their creamy sauce on mash, rice or pasta – the choice is yours.

 2½– 3½ hours 4

- 500g/1lb 2oz lean minced beef
- ½ tbsp olive oil
- 200g/7oz small button mushrooms, thickly sliced
- 1 red onion, sliced
- 1 garlic clove, crushed
- 1 tbsp plain flour
- 1 tbsp sweet paprika
- 1 beef stock cube
- 2 tbsp tomato purée
- 150ml pot soured cream
- small handful flat-leaf parsley, roughly chopped

1 Heat the slow cooker if necessary. Season the beef then shape into about 16-20 walnut-size meatballs. Heat the oil in a non-stick frying pan then fry them until brown on all sides. Tip into the slow cooker pot with the mushrooms.

2 Add the onion and garlic to the pan and cook for a few mins until softened. Stir in the flour and paprika, then add 250ml/9fl oz water with the crumbled stock cube and tomato purée. Stir until thickened, then scrape into the slow cooker pot and stir with the meatballs and mushrooms. Don't worry if it seems a bit dry at the moment as liquid will come from the mushrooms during the cooking process. Cover and cook on Low for 2-3 hours.

3 Stir in the soured cream and most of the parsley and warm through with the lid off for a few mins. Serve scattered with the remaining parsley.

PER SERVING 425 kcals, fat 29g, saturates 14g, carbs 10g, sugars 4g, fibre 2g, protein 30g, salt 1g

Smoky Pork & Boston Beans One-pot

You can use skinless chicken thighs on the bone instead of pork if you prefer. They will take the same time to cook.

 4½ hours 4

- 2 tbsp olive oil
- 2 garlic cloves, crushed
- 2 tbsp smoked paprika
- 500g/1lb 2oz pork shoulder steaks, quartered
- 500g pack passata
- 2 x 400g cans cannellini beans, one can drained
- 1-2 tsp chipotle paste
- 1 tbsp dark soft brown sugar
- 1 tbsp red wine vinegar
- 1 chicken stock cube
- 100g/4oz ham hock, in large shreds
- 4 slices crusty white bread
- small handful flat-leaf parsley, roughly chopped

1 Heat the slow cooker if necessary. Mix the oil, garlic and paprika together and rub into the pork. Heat a non-stick frying pan and seal the pork on both sides then lift from the pan.

2 Pour in the passata, cannellini beans, chipotle, sugar, vinegar crumbled stock cube and ham hock and heat until bubbling. Tip into the slow cooker pot and nestle the pork into the beans. Cover and cook on Low for 4 hours until the pork is tender.

3 Toast the bread and serve on the side. Sprinkle the parsley over the pork and beans to serve.

PER SERVING 475 kcals, fat 15g, saturates 4g, carbs 40g, sugars 12g, fibre 3g, protein 44g, salt 1.8g

Chicken, Butter Bean & Pepper Stew

You can make this with chicken breasts instead, but you'll want to cook it for less time or they will dry out.

 8-9 hours   4

- 1 tbsp olive oil
- 8 chicken thighs, skin removed
- 1 large onion, chopped
- 2 celery sticks, chopped
- 1 yellow and 1 red pepper, deseeded and diced
- 1 garlic clove, crushed
- 2 tbsp paprika
- 400g can chopped tomatoes
- 150ml/¼ pint chicken stock
- 2 x 400g cans butter beans, drained and rinsed

1 Heat the slow cooker if necessary. Heat the oil in a large frying pan and brown the thighs on both sides. Put in the slow cooker pot with the onion, celery, peppers, garlic, paprika, tomatoes and stock. Cover and cook on Low for 7–8 hours until the chicken is really tender.

2 Stir in the butter beans, and season well. Leave uncovered and cook for 30 mins more to heat through.

PER SERVING 422 kcals, fat 15g, saturates 4g, carbs 27g, sugars 12g, fibre 9g, protein 44g, salt 1.6g

Poule au Pot

This simple French dish makes a wonderful Sunday lunch for the family.

 6 hours   6

- 1.5 kg/3lb 5oz whole chicken
- 12 small potatoes, peeled
- 300ml/½ pint white wine
- 1 onion, peeled, but left whole and studded with 3 cloves
- 1 bouquet garni
- 3 garlic cloves, unpeeled
- 4 carrots, cut into 5cm/2in lengths
- 2 turnips, cut into wedges
- 200ml tub crème fraîche
- 3 leeks, cut into 5cm/2in lengths
- roughly chopped parsley, to serve
- stuffing balls, to serve

1 Heat the slow cooker if necessary. Put in the chicken, potatoes, 600ml/1 pint water, wine, clove-studded onion, bouquet garni, garlic and some seasoning. Cover and cook on High for 3 hours.

2 After 2 hours, fish out the garlic. Add the carrots and turnips, turn the chicken over then re-cover and cook on High for another 2 hours. Squeeze the garlic cloves out of their skins and mash with some seasoning. Stir into the crème fraîche, then chill until ready to serve.

3 After the second 2 hours of cooking, add the leeks, and cover and cook on High for another hour, at which point the chicken should be done.

4 Lift out the chicken and veg and reserve one ladle of stock. Pour the rest into a pan and boil to reduce. Remove the chicken's skin and tear the flesh into chunks. Put on a warm platter with the veg and stuffing balls. Add the ladle of stock and the parsley, and serve with the reduced juices and garlic cream.

PER SERVING 745 kcals, fat 37g, saturates 16g, carbs 48g, sugars 14g, fibre 7g, protein 54g, salt 1.31g

Pesto-chicken Stew with Cheesy Dumplings

If you've got a 5-litre slow cooker make the full quantity given here, but otherwise adjust the recipe according to your pot size.

 9½ hours   8

- 2 tbsp olive oil
- 12–15 bone-in chicken thighs, skin removed
- 200g/7oz smoked bacon lardons or chopped bacon rashers
- 4 tbsp plain flour
- 1 large onion, chopped
- 4 celery sticks, chopped
- 3 leeks, chopped
- 140g/5oz each sundried tomatoes and fresh pesto
- 700ml/1¼ pints chicken stock
- small bunch basil, shredded
- 200g/7oz frozen peas

FOR THE DUMPLINGS
- 140g/5oz butter
- 250g/9oz self-raising flour
- 100g/4oz Parmesan, grated
- 50g/2oz pine nuts

1 Heat the slow cooker if necessary. Heat the oil in a large frying pan. Brown the chicken – you might have to do this in batches – and remove to the slow cooker pot as you go. Crisp the bacon in the pan, add to the pot, then stir in the flour.
2 Stir in the onion, celery, leeks, sundried tomatoes, pesto and stock. Cover and cook for 8 hours on Low.
3 Heat oven to 200C/180C fan/gas 6. Transfer to an ovenproof dish if you need to. Stir in the basil and peas, and season.
4 For the dumplings, rub the butter into the flour until it resembles breadcrumbs. Mix in the grated cheese and add 150ml/5fl oz water, mixing with a cutlery knife until it forms a light and sticky dough. Break off walnut-sized lumps and shape into balls. Put the dumplings on top of the stew and scatter with pine nuts. Bake in the oven for 25 mins or until the dumplings are golden brown and cooked through.

PER SERVING 793 kcals, fat 52g, saturates 17g, carbs 38g, sugars 5g, fibre 5g, protein 42g, salt 2.7g

Squash & Chorizo Pot Pies

The chorizo adds a wonderful smoky flavour and, although the contents of these pies are mostly veg, they are very hearty and filling.

 2½–3 hours   4

- 2 red onions, chopped
- 175g/6oz chorizo, skin removed, sliced
- 300g/11oz butternut squash, peeled and cut into cubes
- 400g can chickpeas
- 200g bag spinach
- 140g/5oz crème fraîche
- 320g puff pastry sheets
- 1 egg, beaten

1 Heat the slow cooker if necessary. Put the onions, chorizo, squash and chickpeas with their liquid in the slow cooker pot and pour in 50ml/2fl oz water. Cover and cook on Low for 1½-2 hours until the squash is just cooked through.

2 Turn the switch to High, add the spinach and some seasoning and stir until the spinach has wilted. Stir in the crème fraîche.

3 Heat oven to 200C/180C fan/gas 6. Divide the filling among four pie dishes. Unroll the pastry and cut out four lids, large enough to cover the pies. Brush the edge of each dish with a little beaten egg, then put a pastry lid on top and brush this with egg too. Poke a hole in the top of each pie. Bake on a tray for 25 mins until the lids are puffed and golden.

PER SERVING 735 kcals, fat 47g, saturates 23g, carbs 51g, sugars 10g, fibre 7g, protein 22g, salt 1.9g

Chicken, Leek & Parsley Pie

If you want to make this pie ahead, prepare the filling and cool it, then top with pastry and freeze. Then just defrost the pie overnight and bake as usual.

 6–7 hours 4–6

- 1.5kg/3lb whole chicken
- 1 each carrot, onion and celery stick, roughly chopped
- 1 bouquet garni
- 2 leeks, sliced
- 50g/2oz butter
- 2 tbsp plain flour
- grated zest 1 lemon
- bunch parsley, chopped
- 3 tbsp crème fraîche
- 250g ready-made puff pastry
- little beaten egg, to glaze

1 Heat the slow cooker if necessary. Put the chicken, carrot, onion, celery and bouquet garni in the pot with enough boiling water almost to cover. Cover and cook on High for 5–6 hours until the chicken is cooked through.
2 Lift the chicken on to a plate. Strain the stock, discarding the veggies, and measure out and reserve 500ml/18fl oz.
3 Heat oven to 200C/180C fan/gas 6. Strip the meat from the chicken and put it into a pie dish.
4 Fry the leeks in butter until soft. Stir in the flour, then gradually add the reserved stock, cooking until the sauce is smooth. Add the zest, parsley, crème fraîche and some seasoning. Pour over the chicken.
5 Roll out the pastry on a lightly floured surface and trim to 5cm/2in larger than the dish. Brush the edges of the dish with water and lay on the pastry, tucking the edges under to make a double layer around the rim. Press the pastry edges to seal. Brush with the beaten egg and bake for 30–35 mins.

PER SERVING (6) 401 kcals, fat 23g, saturates 10g, carbs 21g, sugars 2g, fibre 1g, protein 28g, salt 0.60g

Easy One-pot Chicken

This make a very quick and easy family meal in one. Serve with a knife, fork and spoon for the sauce, or mash the potatoes into the sauce as you eat it.

 4½ hours 4

- 8 bone-in chicken thighs, skin removed
- 1 tbsp sunflower oil
- 2 large carrots, cut into batons
- 400g/14oz new potatoes, halved if large
- 5 spring onions, sliced, white and green parts kept separate
- 2 tbsp plain flour
- 2 chicken stock cubes
- 1 tbsp grainy or Dijon mustard
- 200g/7oz frozen peas
- small pack fresh soft herbs, like parsley, chives or tarragon, chopped (optional)

1 Heat the slow cooker if necessary. Put the kettle on. Fry the thighs in the oil in a large non-stick frying pan to brown them. Put them in the slow cooker pot with the carrots and potatoes.

2 Stir the whites of the spring onion into the chicken pan juices with the flour, crumble in the stock cubes and stir for 1-2 mins. Gradually stir in 600ml/1 pint hot water from the kettle, bring the boil, stirring, then pour into the slow cooker pot. Stir to mix, then cover and cook on Low for 3½ hours.

3 Take off the lid and quickly stir in the mustard, peas and spring onion tops, then cover and cook for 40 mins more. Add the herbs, if using, and some seasoning to taste before serving.

PER SERVING 386 kcals, fat 10g, saturates 2g, carbs 32g, sugars 8g, fibre 6g, protein 43g, salt 2.1g

Salsa Chicken Peppers

These peppers make a lovely lunch with a green salad and are a great way to use up any leftover chicken from dinner the night before.

 3 hours   4-6    easily halved

- 140g/5oz Camargue red rice or brown basmati rice
- 6 large red peppers
- oil, for brushing
- 270g jar hot salsa
- 200g/7oz cooked chicken, chopped
- 215g can red kidney beans, drained and rinsed
- 40g/1½oz mature cheddar, grated
- 20g pack coriander, chopped
- lime wedges, to garnish

1 Boil the rice for 25 mins, or following the pack instructions, until just tender. Meanwhile, heat the slow cooker if necessary. Slice the tops off the peppers and cut out and discard the seeds. Set aside the peppers and their tops, then oil the base of the slow cooker pot.

2 Drain the rice and mix with the salsa, chicken, beans, cheddar and coriander. Season to taste. Fill the peppers with the rice mixture. Put on the tops, then sit the stuffed peppers in the slow cooker and cover with the lid. Cook for 2 hours on High until the peppers are tender. Squeeze over lime wedges and serve with an avocado salad.

PER SERVING (4) 370 kcals, fat 10g, saturates 4g, carbs 50g, sugars 15g, fibre 5g, protein 24g, salt 1.65g

Summer Roast Chicken

The vinaigrette in this dish is a delicious alternative to gravy, making it a perfect dish in the summer when you fancy something lighter than a traditional roast.

 6 hours   4

- 50g/2oz unsalted butter, softened
- juice ½ lemon
- small bunch sage, leaves only, roughly chopped
- 1.6kg/3lb 8oz whole chicken
- 1 head garlic, broken into cloves in the skins
- 7 tbsp olive oil
- 600g/1lb 5oz small potatoes, scrubbed, cut in half if large
- 300ml/½ pint chicken stock
- 4 large courgettes, cut into large chunks
- 2 red peppers, halved and deseeded
- 200g/7oz baby plum tomatoes, skin slashed with a knife
- 1 tbsp red wine vinegar

1 Heat the slow cooker if necessary. Mash the butter, lemon juice, sage and some seasoning. Separate the skin from the chicken breast using your hand – being careful not to break the skin. Rub the butter underneath and stuff the cavity with half the garlic. Fry the chicken in 4 tablespoons of the oil in a large frying pan until browned all over. Transfer to the slow cooker pot breast-side down. Stir the potatoes into the pan, frying until golden, then scrape into the pot too. Add the stock, season, then cover and cook on High for 4 hours.

2 Turn the chicken over and add the courgettes, pushing them under the chicken so they are covered in the stock. Fill the pepper halves with tomatoes and add these to the pot with the remaining garlic. Cover and cook for another hour until the chicken is done. Transfer to a serving dish to rest, covered with foil. Tip the pot juices into a pan, bubble until reduced by half, stir in the remaining oil and the vinegar, and serve.

PER SERVING 962 kcals, fat 65g, saturates 28g, carbs 36g, sugars 9g, fibre 5g, protein 60g, salt 0.73g

Saucy Chicken & Spring Vegetables

Add a spoon of grainy mustard to the sauce with the crème fraîche if you like it tangy.

 3 hours   2

- 2 chicken breasts, skin on
- 1 tbsp olive oil
- 200g/7oz baby new potatoes, thinly sliced
- 250ml/9fl oz chicken stock
- 200g pack mixed spring veg (broccoli, peas, broad beans and sliced courgettes)
- 2 tbsp crème fraîche
- handful tarragon leaves, roughly chopped

1 Heat the slow cooker if necessary. Fry the chicken, skin-side down, in the oil in a frying pan for 5 mins to brown. Turn the chicken over, throw in the potatoes and stir to coat. Spread the potatoes over the bottom of the slow cooker pot, then sit the chicken on top. Pour over the stock then cover and cook on High for 1½ hours.
2 Remove the chicken and stir in the veg, then pop the chicken back on top, cover and cook for another hour until the chicken and potatoes are cooked through.
3 Stir in the crème fraîche to make a creamy sauce, season with pepper and salt, if you want, then add the tarragon. If you like a thicker sauce, scoop out the chicken and veg with a slotted spoon and reduce the sauce by bubbling it in the frying pan.

PER SERVING 386 kcals, fat 16g, saturates 6g, carbs 23g, sugars 24g, fibre 3g, protein 38g, salt 1.5g

Stickiest-ever BBQ Ribs

Is there anything nicer than sticky ribs? We think so – ribs cooked in a slow cooker so they are meltingly tender and falling off the bone, then simply crisped up to serve.

🕐 6–8 hours, plus marinating　　◔ 4 (or 8 with other BBQ food)

- 2 racks baby back pork ribs
- 2 x 330ml cans cola
- 8 tbsp tomato ketchup
- 8 tbsp brown sugar
- 2 tbsp soy sauce
- 2 tbsp Worcestershire sauce
- 2 tbsp sweet chilli sauce
- 1 tsp paprika
- 2 tsp toasted sesame seeds, to garnish (optional)

1 Heat the slow cooker if necessary. Cut the ribs into small racks so they fit into your slow cooker pot. Pour over the cola and enough water to cover the ribs, then cover and cook on High for 5–7 hours, until they are tender but not falling apart.

2 Meanwhile, put the sauce ingredients in a small pan. Gently heat, then bubble for about 2 mins, stirring.

3 When the ribs are done, carefully lift on to kitchen paper to dry. Transfer to a roasting tin and coat with the sauce. Cover and chill for 1-24 hours to marinate.

4 Heat the barbecue or heat oven to 220C/200C fan/gas 7. Add the ribs (in the roasting tin, if using the oven) and cook for 20 mins, turning occasionally, and basting often with the remaining sauce. When the ribs are hot through and crisping on the outside, slice to serve. Scatter with the sesame seeds, if you like, and serve with any remaining sauce.

PER SERVING (8) 450 kcals, fat 23g, saturates 9g, carbs 37g, sugars 35g, fibre none, protein 25g, salt 2g

Lancashire Hotpot

Everybody loves Lancashire hotpot with its crispy potato topping and it's even easier to make when you've got a slow cooker.

 5-6 hours   4

- 5 tbsp lard or olive oil
- 900g/2lb stewing lamb, cut into large chunks
- 2 medium onions, chopped
- 4 carrots, sliced
- 50g/2oz plain flour
- 2 tsp Worcestershire sauce
- 300ml/½ pint lamb or chicken stock
- 2 bay leaves
- 2 thyme sprigs
- 900g/2lb potatoes, peeled and sliced

1 Heat the slow cooker if necessary. Heat 3 tablespoons of the lard or oil in a large frying pan and brown the lamb in batches.

2 Fry the onions and carrots in the pan with 1 tablespoon more of the lard or oil until golden. Stir in the flour and allow to cook for a couple of mins. Tip into the slow cooker pot with the lamb, Worcestershire sauce, stock, bay, thyme and some seasoning. Give everything a good stir, then push down evenly in the pot. Arrange the sliced potatoes on top of the meat, then dot with the remaining lard or drizzle with the rest of the oil. Sprinkle over a little more seasoning, cover, and cook on High for 4–5 hours until the lamb and potatoes are tender.

3 If you like, finish the dish under the grill for 5–8 mins until the potatoes are browned and crisp.

PER SERVING 891 kcals, fat 48g, saturates 23g, carbs 60g, sugars 11g, fibre 6g, protein 59g, salt 0.93g

Slow-cooked Irish Stew

Middle neck or scrag-end of lamb are flavoursome cuts and perfect for braising. This traditional casserole contains filling pearl barley, too.

🕐 7½–8½ hours   🥧 6

- 1 tbsp sunflower oil
- 200g/7oz smoked streaky bacon, preferably in one piece, skinned and cut into chunks
- 900g/1lb 15oz cheap stewing lamb, such as middle neck or scrag-end (ask at your butcher counter), cut into large chunks
- small bunch thyme
- 3 onions, thickly sliced
- 5 carrots, cut into big chunks
- 6 medium potatoes, cut into big chunks
- 700ml/1¼ pints lamb stock
- 3 bay leaves
- 85g/3oz pearl barley
- 1 large leek, washed and cut into chunks
- small knob butter

1 Heat the slow cooker if necessary, then heat the oil in a frying pan. Sizzle the bacon until crisp, tip into the slow cooker pot, then brown the chunks of lamb in the pan in batches. Transfer to the slow cooker pot along with the thyme, onions, carrots, potatoes, stock, bay leaves and enough water to cover the lamb. Cover and cook on Low for 6–7 hours.

2 Stir in the pearl barley and leek and then cook on High for 1 hour more until the pearl barley is tender.

3 Stir in the butter, season and serve scooped straight from the dish.

PER SERVING 673 kcals, fat 39g, saturates 16g, carbs 40g, sugars 11g, fibre 7g, protein 40g, salt 1.4g

Minced Beef & Sweet Potato Stew

You can make this with lamb mince too if you like, or even half lamb mince, half beef mince if you've got bits to use up.

 7–9 hours 4

- 1 tbsp sunflower oil
- 500g/1lb 2oz lean minced beef
- 1 large onion, chopped
- 1 large carrot, chopped
- 1 celery stick, sliced
- 1 tbsp each tomato purée and mushroom ketchup
- 400g can chopped tomatoes
- 450g/1lb sweet potatoes, peeled and cut into large chunks
- few thyme sprigs
- 1 bay leaf
- handful parsley, chopped
- shredded and steamed Savoy cabbage, to serve

1 Heat your slow cooker if necessary. Heat the oil in a large frying pan, add the beef and cook until it is browned all over.

2 Put the mince in your slow cooker pot with the onion, carrot, celery, tomato purée, mushroom ketchup, chopped tomatoes, sweet potatoes, thyme, bay leaf and 200ml/7fl oz water. Season, cover and then cook on Low for 6–8 hours until the mince and potatoes are tender.

3 Once cooked, remove the bay leaf, stir through the chopped parsley and serve with the shredded and steamed cabbage.

PER SERVING 368 kcals, fat 13g, saturates 5g, carbs 35g, sugars 17g, fibre 6g, protein 29g, salt 0.6g

Sustainable Fish Pie

To prepare ahead, make the filling and mash, assemble, then cool and chill for up to 24 hours. To serve, heat oven to 180C/160C fan/gas 4 and bake for 30–40 minutes.

 4½ hours 6

- 400ml/14fl oz full-fat milk
- 50g/2oz butter, plus extra for dotting
- 50g/2oz plain flour
- 1 onion, finely chopped
- 2 bay leaves
- good grating nutmeg
- 700g/1lb 9oz pollock fillet, skinned and cut into bite-sized pieces
- 300g/10oz raw peeled North Atlantic prawns
- small bunch parsley, chopped

FOR THE MASH
- 1kg/2lb 4oz floury potatoes, peeled and chopped into chunks
- 50ml/2fl oz full-fat milk
- 25g/1oz butter
- pinch freshly grated nutmeg

1 Heat your slow cooker if necessary. Heat the milk in a pan until just about to boil. Mix the butter and flour to a paste in the slow cooker pot, then gradually whisk in the milk to a smooth sauce. Stir in the onion, bay leaves and nutmeg with some seasoning. Cover and cook on High for 3 hours, stirring every hour.

2 Add the fish, prawns and parsley, and cook on High for 30 minutes more until the fish and prawns are just cooked.

3 While the fish cooks, boil the potatoes until cooked, then drain well. Put the pan over the heat again, add the milk, butter and nutmeg, and mash until smooth. Season well.

4 Heat the grill. Spoon the mash on to the fish mixture – after transferring the fish mixture to an ovenproof dish if you need to. Dot the pie with butter, then grill until golden on top.

PER SERVING 435 kcals, fat 16g, saturates 9g, carbs 37g, sugars 6g, fibre 3g, protein 36g, salt 0.9g

Creamy Smoked Haddock Kedgeree

Use good-quality undyed smoked haddock in this creamy brunch rice dish with hard-boiled eggs, parsley and saffron.

 3 hours 4

- 300g/10oz basmati rice
- 50g/2oz butter
- 3 eggs
- 100ml/3½fl oz white wine
- 600ml/1 pint hot vegetable or fish stock
- 1 tsp cayenne pepper
- pinch saffron threads
- 1 tbsp mild curry powder
- a little freshly grated nutmeg
- 200ml/7fl oz double cream
- 500g/1lb 2oz naturally smoked haddock fillet, skin removed
- small handful flat-leaf parsley, chopped
- 1 lemon, cut into wedges, to garnish

1 Heat the slow cooker if necessary. Put the rice, butter, eggs (in their shells), wine, stock and spices into the slow cooker pot and cook on High for 2 hours.
2 Fish the eggs out of the pan and set aside. Stir the cream into the rice, put the haddock on top, cover and cook for a further 30 mins.
3 Peel the eggs and roughly chop. Stir through the rice with the parsley and serve with lemon wedges on the side.

PER SERVING 424 kcals, fat 30g, saturates 16g, carbs 17g, sugars 2g, fibre 1g, protein 22g, salt 2.15g

Easy Paella

This is a cheat's version of the Spanish favourite. Serve with crusty bread and a glass of something cold.

 3 hours   4

- 1 tbsp olive oil
- 1 onion, chopped
- 1 tsp each hot smoked paprika and dried thyme
- 300g/10oz paella or risotto rice, rinsed until the water runs clear
- 3 tbsp dry Sherry or white wine (optional)
- 400g can chopped tomatoes with garlic
- 900ml/1½ pints chicken stock
- 400g bag frozen mixed seafood
- juice ½ lemon, other half cut into wedges, to garnish
- handful flat-leaf parsley, roughly chopped, to scatter
- crusty bread, to serve

1 Heat the slow cooker if necessary. Heat the oil in a large frying pan. Add the onion and soften for 5 mins. Stir in the paprika, thyme and rice, stir for 1 min, then splash in the Sherry or wine, if using. Once it has evaporated, scrape everything into the slow cooker pot. Stir in the tomatoes and stock. Season, cover and cook on High for about 2 hours.

2 Stir the frozen seafood into the pot, cover and cook for another 30 mins or until the prawns are cooked through and the rice is tender. Squeeze over the lemon juice, scatter with parsley and serve with extra lemon wedges.

PER SERVING 431 kcals, fat 5g, saturates 1g, carbs 66g, sugars 5g, fibre 3g, protein 34g, salt 2.14g

Chapter 3:

CASEROLES, SPICY STEWS & CURRIES

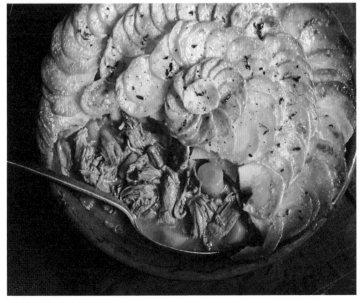

Chicken, Bacon & Potato Stew

A pot of buttermilk is added at the end of cooking to this, so make sure your sauce isn't too thin before stirring it in. Serve with something fresh on the side like broccoli, peas or greens.

 5-7 hours 6

- 1 tbsp olive oil
- 6 bone-in chicken thighs, skin removed
- 12 rashers smoked streaky bacon, chopped
- 200g/7oz shallots
- 350g/12oz baby new potatoes, larger ones halved
- few thyme sprigs
- 200ml/7fl oz white wine
- 500ml/18fl oz hot chicken stock
- 280ml pot buttermilk (optional)
- squeeze lemon juice
- 2 tbsp tarragon, chopped

1 Heat the slow cooker if necessary. Heat the oil in a large saucepan and brown the chicken thighs for about 10 mins, until they have a nice golden colour, then remove and set aside. Add the bacon and shallots to the pan, and brown these, too.

2 Tip everything apart from the buttermilk, lemon juice and 1 tablespoon tarragon into your slow cooker. Cover and simmer on High for 4-6 hours, until the chicken is really tender and falling off the bone.

3 Check the sauce and if you like it a little thicker, strain it into a pan and boil until thickened then return it to the pot. Stir in the buttermilk, if using. Sprinkle in the lemon juice and remaining tarragon before serving.

PER SERVING 284 kcals, fat 13g, saturates 4g, carbs 12g, sugars 4g, fibre 2g, protein 2g, salt 1.7g

One-pot Chicken with Chorizo & New Potatoes

This easy one-pot chicken is given a Spanish accent from Sherry and another of the nation's favourite ingredients, chorizo.

 5½-6 hours, plus resting 4

- 1.5kg/3lb 5oz whole chicken
- small knob of butter
- 1 tbsp olive oil
- ½ lemon
- 1 bay leaf
- few thyme sprigs
- 300g/11oz chorizo ring, thickly sliced
- 700g/1lb 9oz new potatoes, halved (or quartered if really large)
- 12 garlic cloves, left whole and unpeeled
- large splash of dry Sherry
- 300ml/½ pint chicken stock
- handful parsley leaves, roughly chopped

1 Heat the slow cooker if necessary and season the chicken all over. In a large frying pan, heat the butter and oil until sizzling, then brown the chicken well all over. Remove from the dish and pop the lemon, bay and half the thyme in the cavity. Put the chicken, breast side down, inside the slow cooker pot.

2 Pour most of the oil out of the frying pan, place back on the heat and sizzle the chorizo for 5 mins until it starts to release its red oil. Throw in the potatoes, sizzle them until they start to colour, then add the garlic and remaining thyme. Splash in the Sherry, then pour in the stock.

3 Tip into the slow cooker while it is still bubbling, cover and cook on Low for 4½ –5 hours until the legs easily come away from the body. Leave the chicken to rest for 10 mins, then scatter with parsley and serve straight from the pot.

PER SERVING 791 kcals, fat 44g, saturates 15g, carbs 32g, sugars 5g, fibre 3g, protein 65g, salt 1.6g

Chicken & Red Wine Casserole with Herby Dumplings

If this sauce tastes too strongly of wine for you, then before you add it to the slow cooker pot boil it in a pan to burn off the alcohol kick.

 5½-7½ hours 6

- 3 tbsp olive oil
- 6 chicken breasts, halved
- 3 tbsp plain flour
- 3 onions, each peeled and cut into 8 wedges
- 200g/7oz smoked bacon lardons
- 3 garlic cloves, peeled and sliced
- 300g/10oz large flat mushrooms, sliced
- 2 tbsp redcurrant sauce
- 300ml/½ pint each red wine and chicken stock

FOR THE DUMPLINGS
- 100g/4oz each self-raising flour and fresh white breadcrumbs
- 1 tbsp wholegrain mustard
- 140g/5oz butter, cubed
- 2 tsp thyme leaves, plus extra to garnish
- 2 tbsp chopped parsley
- 2 medium eggs, lightly beaten

1 Heat the slow cooker if necessary. Heat the oil in a frying pan and, in batches, brown the chicken. Transfer to the slow cooker pot with the flour, onions, lardons, garlic, mushrooms, redcurrant sauce, red wine and stock, and season. Cover and cook on High for 4 hours.

2 After 3½ hours of cooking, make the dumplings. Put the flour, crumbs, mustard and butter in a food processor and whizz to crumbs. Add the thyme, parsley, eggs and some seasoning, and work together to make a moist dough. Using floured hands, roll the mixture into six balls.

3 Remove the lid after 4 hours and sit the dumplings on top of the casserole. Cover and cook for 1–2 hours until the chicken is tender and the dumplings have puffed up. Serve scattered with the extra thyme leaves.

PER SERVING 701 kcals, fat 37g, saturates 17g, carbs 38g, sugars 1g, fibre 3g, protein 47g, salt 2.55g

Chicken Arrabbiata

The name actually means 'angry' – and just like the pasta sauce, this dish is intended to pack quite a punch.

 8½–9½ hours   6

- 350ml/12fl oz red wine
- 3 tbsp olive oil
- 2 medium onions, halved and sliced
- 1 garlic bulb, separated into cloves
- 2 red chillies, deseeded and sliced
- 150ml/¼ pint chicken stock
- 600g/1lb 5oz tomatoes, finely chopped
- 3 tbsp tomato purée
- 2 tsp chopped thyme leaves
- 6 chicken legs, skin removed
- chopped parsley, to garnish (optional)
- pasta or mashed potato, to serve

1 Heat the slow cooker if necessary. Put the wine in a small pan and bring to a simmer. Let it bubble for a minute then pour it into the slow cooker pot and stir in the olive oil, onions, garlic cloves, chillies, stock, tomatoes, tomato purée and thyme with some seasoning. Add the chicken legs, pushing them under the liquid, then cover the pan and cook on Low for 8–9 hours until the chicken is tender.

2 Serve scattered with parsley, if you like, and pasta or mashed potato.

PER SERVING 327 kcals, fat 13g, saturates 3g, carbs 9g, sugars 7g, fibre 3g, protein 35g, salt 0.5g

Beef in Red Wine with Melting Onions

Beef skirt and shin are underused cuts that are great value, and particularly delicious after slow cooking.

 5½ hours 4-6  easily doubled

- 25g/1oz butter
- 2 large onions, sliced into rings
- 6 garlic cloves, halved
- 250g mushrooms, halved (we used small Portobello mushrooms)
- 3 tbsp plain flour
- 600g/1lb 5oz piece beef skirt or slices of shin, cut into large chunks
- 2 tbsp olive oil
- 3 bay leaves
- 400ml/14fl oz red wine
- 1 tbsp tomato purée
- 1 beef stock cube
- chopped parsley, to serve (optional)

1 Heat the slow cooker if necessary. In a large pan, melt the butter over a medium heat. Add the onions and garlic, fry for 10 mins until starting to brown, then transfer to the slow cooker pot with the mushrooms.
2 Put the flour on a plate with plenty of black pepper. Add the beef and toss in the flour to coat it.
3 Heat the oil in the same pan you cooked the onions in (there's no need to clean it first). Add the beef and bay leaves, and fry until the meat is browned all over. Put in the pot with the mushrooms.
4 Pour the wine into the pan, add the tomato purée and stock cube then stir until bubbling. Pour into the slow cooker, cover and cook on Low for 5 hours until the meat is tender. Serve scattered with parsley, if you like.

PER SERVING (6) 360 kcals, fat 19g, saturates 7g, carbs 15g, sugars 5g, fibre 3g, protein 20g, salt 0.4g

Braised Oxtail with Basil Dumplings

Oxtail is tough, so cooking it in a slow cooker couldn't be more convenient – although you do need a large one. What you are left with is soft, melting meat with a glistening sauce.

 9½-10½ hours 6

- 2 tbsp plain flour
- 2 already jointed oxtails
- 4 tbsp sunflower oil, for frying
- 2 onions, chopped
- 3 carrots, cut into small chunks
- 2 celery sticks, cut into small chunks
- 2 garlic cloves, chopped
- 2 tbsp tomato purée
- 2 bay leaves and thyme sprigs, tied together
- 1 bottle full-bodied red wine
- 400ml/14fl oz beef stock
- basil leaves, to serve

FOR THE DUMPLINGS (OPTIONAL)
- 300g/11oz self-raising flour
- bunch basil, leaves removed
- 75g/2½oz butter
- 3 egg whites
- olive oil, for drizzling

1 Heat the slow cooker if necessary. Season the flour with salt and pepper, then toss the oxtail in it until evenly coated. Heat the oil in a large flameproof casserole. Working in batches, brown the meat really well on all sides. Remove from the pan and put in the slow cooker pot.

2 Add the veg and garlic to the pan and fry for 3-4 mins until starting to colour. Stir in the tomato purée and herbs, pour over the wine and stock and bring to the boil. Season, pour into the slow cooker then cover and cook on Low for 8-9 hours until the meat is really tender. If you are making this ahead, chill in the fridge and lift any fat off the top before reheating, otherwise skim off now with a spoon. Check the consistency of the sauce before serving and pour off and reduce it in a frying pan if necessary.

3 If making the dumplings, tip the flour and basil (reserving a few leaves for a garnish) into a food processor with a generous pinch of salt, then blitz until the basil is finely chopped. Add the butter and blitz until it's the texture of breadcrumbs, then gradually add the egg whites until everything comes together. On a floured surface, roll the dumplings into small, walnut-size balls, then cover with a tea towel until ready to cook.

4 To serve, bring a large pan of salted water to the boil. Simmer the dumplings for 15 mins, then remove with a slotted spoon. While the dumplings are cooking, gently reheat the meat in the sauce. Serve a few chunks of meat in a soup bowl with a few dumplings, drizzled with olive oil and scattered with a few basil leaves.

PER SERVING 812 kcals, fat 41g, saturates 17g, carbs 50g, sugars 8g, fibre 4g, protein 53g, salt 2.08g

Lamb & Dauphinoise Hotpot

You know how delicious those last few forkfuls of a large roast are when all the different components have melted into the gravy? Well, every mouthful of this pie tastes just like that.

 10-11 hours, plus overnight chilling   8

- 3 large carrots, cut into large chunks
- 1 onion, roughly chopped
- 2kg/4lb 8oz shoulder of lamb on the bone, but without the thin leg joint attached
- 1 bottle red wine
- 1 garlic bulb, cloves peeled
- few sprigs each rosemary and thyme
- 2 bay leaves
- 2 tbsp tomato purée

FOR THE TOPPING
- 4-5 potatoes and 4 sweet potatoes (the roundest you have), peeled and sliced
- 150ml pot double cream
- few knobs of butter

1 Heat the slow cooker if necessary. Pile the carrots and onion into the slow cooker pot – it needs to be a large cooker – then put the lamb on top. Tip the wine, garlic herbs and tomato purée into a pan with seasoning and heat until bubbling, stirring to dissolve the purée.

2 Pour into the slow cooker, cover with baking parchment and then the lid, then cook on Low for 8-9 hours until the meat is really tender. If there is a lot of liquid, boil it in a frying pan to reduce it. Tip back over the meat, cool then chill overnight.

3 The next day, remove all the hard fat from around the lamb and discard. Lift the lamb out of the pot, scraping away and keeping the jellified juices. Pull apart and shred the meat, discarding any large pieces of fat and the bones. Put the lamb in a large ovenproof dish, then spoon over the jellied sauce and mix with the vegetables. Set aside.

4 Heat oven to 200C/180C fan/gas 6. To make the topping, place the potatoes and sweet potatoes in a pan of cold salted water, bring to a hard boil and drain straight away.

5 Tip back in the pan, pour over the cream and season. Arrange the potato and sweet potato in interleaving circles on top of the lamb, drizzle over any remaining cream from the pan and dot with the butter. Bake for 40 mins-1 hour until the top is golden and the sauce is just starting to bubble.

PER SERVING 645 kcals, fat 32g, saturates 17g, carbs 24g, sugars 9g, fibre 4g, protein 49g, salt 0.6g

Chorizo, Pork Belly & Chickpea Casserole

A bread-moppingly-good one-pot full of hearty flavours and tender chunks of pork.

 6-7 hours 4

- 1 tbsp olive oil
- 700g/1lb 9oz skinless, boneless pork belly, cut into large bite-sized chunks 100g/4oz cooking chorizo, sliced into thin rounds
- 1 large onion, chopped
- 1 large carrot, finely chopped
- 1 tsp fennel seeds
- small pinch of dried chilli flakes
- 2 garlic cloves
- 4 bay leaves (fresh are best)
- 2 thyme sprigs
- large pinch caster sugar
- 1 tbsp tomato purée
- 50ml/2fl oz Sherry vinegar or good-quality red wine vinegar
- 400g can chopped tomatoes
- 400g can chickpeas, drained and rinsed
- small pack parsley, chopped

1 Heat the slow cooker if necessary. Heat the oil in a large frying pan and brown the pork on all sides. Scoop the pork out, and put in the slow cooker pot.

2 Add the chorizo to the pan and sizzle for 1 min, then stir in the vegetables, fennel seeds, chilli flakes, garlic, bay leaves and thyme. Cook for about 5 mins until the vegetables are just starting to colour. Sprinkle over the sugar, stir in the tomato purée, then splash in the vinegar and bubble for a moment. Pour in the tomatoes, chickpeas and half a can of water, and bring to the boil.

3 Tip into the slow cooker pot and give it all a good stir. Cover and cook on Low for 5-6 hours until the pork is tender. Stir through the parsley and taste for seasoning before serving.

PER SERVING 680 kcals, fat 45g, saturates 16g, carbs 23g, sugars 9g, fibre 4g, protein 44g, salt 1.3g

Slow-braised Pork Shoulder with Cider & Parsnips

Pork shoulder is the ideal cut for this warming one-pot, as it's not too fatty and not too lean.

 9–10 hours 5

- 2 tbsp olive oil
- 1kg/2lb 4oz pork shoulder, diced
- 2 onions, sliced
- 2 celery sticks, roughly chopped
- 3 parsnips, cut into chunks
- 2 bay leaves
- 1 tbsp plain flour
- 330ml bottle cider
- 450ml/¾ pint chicken stock
- handful parsley, chopped, to garnish
- mashed potato and greens, to serve (optional)

1 Heat the slow cooker if necessary. Heat the oil in a large frying pan and brown the meat in batches, then transfer to the slow cooker pot. Add the onions, celery, parsnips and bay leaves. Sprinkle in the flour and give it a good stir until the flour disappears.

2 Add the cider and stock so that the meat and vegetables are covered. Season, then cover and cook for 8–9 hours on Low. Serve sprinkled with parsley, with mashed potato and greens, if you like.

PER SERVING 534 kcals, fat 29g, saturates 9g, carbs 19g, sugars 10g, fibre 8g, protein 46g, salt 0.8g

Squash & Venison Tagine

You need to make your own spice paste for this, but it is easy if you have a small food processor, if not grind in a large pestle and mortar.

 5 hours 4

FOR THE SPICE PASTE
- 1 tbsp each cumin and coriander seeds
- 1 tsp black peppercorns
- 1 cinnamon stick
- 2 cloves
- bunch coriander, stalks roughly chopped, leaves picked
- thumb-sized piece ginger, peeled and roughly chopped
- 3 garlic cloves, crushed
- 1 fat red chilli, deseeded and roughly chopped

FOR THE TAGINE
- 2-3 tbsp sunflower oil
- 250g/9oz shallots, halved
- 600g/1lb 5oz butternut squash, peeled, seeds removed and cut into large pieces
- 450g/1lb stewing venison (shoulder or shin is best), cut into large pieces
- good pinch of saffron
- 500ml/18fl oz chicken stock
- 8 pitted prunes, halved
- 2 tbsp pomegranate molasses
- bulghar, quinoa or brown rice, to serve
- plain yogurt, to serve

1 First make the spice paste. Heat a frying pan and tip in the cumin, coriander seeds, peppercorns, cinnamon stick and cloves. Warm the spices through, stirring them around from time to time, until they turn a shade darker and smell aromatic. Put the cinnamon stick to one side for later, and tip the remaining spices into the small bowl of a food processor. Whizz to a powder. Add the coriander stalks, ginger, garlic, chilli and 1 tsp salt, and blend to a paste with a little water.

2 Heat the slow cooker if necessary. Heat 1 tablespoon of the oil in a large pan, add the shallots and cook until starting to colour. Lift out and put in the slow cooker pot with the squash.

3 Add the remaining oil to the pan and brown the venison – you'll need to do this in batches so that you don't overcrowd the pan. Take your time, ensuring the meat has a nice dark-brown crust before you remove it from the pan – this will give the tagine a good rich flavour.

4 When all the venison pieces have been browned, return the meat to the pan with the cinnamon stick. Stir in the spice paste and sizzle for 1-2 mins, splashing in a little water if the paste starts to stick to the bottom of the pan. Add the saffron and pour in the stock. Cover and cook on Low for 3 hours.

5 Add the prunes and pomegranate with some seasoning and cook for 1 hour more. Stir through the coriander leaves and serve with your favourite grain – and a dollop of yogurt.

PER SERVING 331 kcals, fat 11g, saturates 2g, carbs 21g, sugars 15g, fibre 6g, protein 33g, salt 1.8g

Brazilian Pork Stew with Corn Dumplings

A Brazilian Feijoada, or stew, has a mixture of different pork products, from spicy sausages to chunks of ham. So if you have any leftover chorizo, ham or bacon, by all means throw it in!

 5 hours   6

- 2 tbsp sunflower oil
- 900g/2lb pork shoulder, cut into large chunks
- 400g/14oz sweet potatoes, peeled and cut into chunks
- 2 red peppers, deseeded and cut into chunks
- 2 onions and 2 celery sticks, finely chopped
- 3 bay leaves
- 1 tbsp oregano leaves (or 2 tsp dried), plus extra, to serve
- 1 tbsp each ground cumin, coriander and allspice
- 1 chicken stock cube
- 2 x 400g cans chopped tomatoes
- 1 tbsp cocoa
- 2 tbsp each soft dark brown sugar and red wine vinegar
- zest and juice 1 orange
- 1-2 red chillies, halved lengthways and deseeded
- 2 x 400g cans black beans, drained and rinsed

FOR THE DUMPLINGS
- 100g/4oz cold butter, diced
- 200g/7oz self-raising flour
- 140g/5oz cornmeal or finely ground polenta, plus extra for dusting
- ½ tsp bicarbonate of soda
- 140g/5oz sweetcorn, from a can, drained,
- 75ml/2½fl oz buttermilk
- 1 medium egg, beaten

1 Heat the slow cooker if necessary. Heat the oil in a large frying pan and seal the pork in batches, then transfer to the slow cooker pot with the sweet potatoes and peppers. Add the onions, the celery, bay and oregano into the pan. Add a splash more oil, if you need to, and fry gently until softened.

2 Tip in the spices, and stir for 1 min to toast. Crumble in the stock cube and stir in the tomatoes, cocoa, sugar, vinegar, the orange zest and juice and chilli halves. Bring to a simmer. Pour into the slow cooker and stir well. Cover and cook on Low for 4 hours.

3 When the stew has about 15 mins to go, make the dumplings. Rub the butter into the flour until it resembles fine crumbs, then stir in the cornmeal, bicarbonate of soda, sweetcorn and a little salt. Mix in the buttermilk and all but 1 tablespoon of the egg to make a soft dough. Roll the mixture into 12 soft dumplings, then roll in a little more cornmeal to coat the tops. Brush the tops with the reserved beaten egg.

4 Heat oven to 200C/180C fan/gas 6. Tip the stew into a large open ovenproof dish and stir in the beans, then taste for seasoning.

5 Sit 6 of the dumplings on top of the stew and the rest on a baking tray lined with baking parchment. Put both in the oven – the stew without a lid – and cook for 25 mins until the dumplings are golden and risen. Carry the stew straight to the table, and sprinkle over a little more oregano before spooning into bowls. Serve the extra dumplings alongside for those who fancy another one.

PER SERVING 886 kcals, fat 33g, saturates 14 g, carbs 95g, sugars 26g, fibre 14g, protein 44g, salt 1.9 g

Sticky Spiced Lamb Shanks

These aromatic lamb shanks are a real treat for two. Serve with fragrant rice or couscous, or some lovely warm flatbreads.

 10–11 hours   2    easily doubled

- 1½ tbsp olive oil
- 2 lamb shanks
- 3 onions, sliced
- 4 garlic cloves, sliced
- ½ cinnamon stick
- 1 tbsp each cumin and coriander seeds, crushed
- pinch chilli flakes
- 400g can chopped tomatoes
- 500ml/18fl oz chicken or vegetable stock
- 2 tbsp pomegranate molasses
- 4 dried apricots, chopped
- 4 dried figs, chopped
- handful coriander, chopped

1 Heat the slow cooker if necessary. Heat the oil in a pan and brown the shanks for a couple of minutes, turning them as you go. Put in the slow cooker pot with all the remaining ingredients except the coriander. Cover and cook on Low for 9–10 hours until the lamb is really tender.
2 Remove the shanks from the pot and wrap in foil to keep warm. Tip the contents of the pot into a pan and boil down the juices until thick and saucy. Season, then serve the shanks scattered with coriander.

PER SERVING 1,114 kcals, fat 55g, saturates 23g, carbs 64g, sugars 52g, fibre 10g, protein 95g, salt 1.93g

Cape Malay Chicken Curry with Yellow Rice

Cape Malay cooking comes from a community in South Africa with its historic roots in South-east Asia. The yellow rice is well worth the effort, but plain basmati will do too.

 3½ hours   6

FOR THE CURRY
- 2 tbsp sunflower oil
- 1 onion, finely chopped
- 4 garlic cloves, finely grated
- 2 tbsp finely grated ginger
- 5 cloves
- 2 tsp turmeric
- 1 tsp each ground white pepper, coriander and cumin
- seeds from 8 cardamom pods, lightly crushed
- 1 cinnamon stick, halved
- 1 large red chilli, halved, deseeded and sliced
- 400g can chopped tomatoes
- 2 tbsp mango chutney
- 1 chicken stock cube
- 12 bone-in chicken thighs, skin removed
- 500g/1lb 2oz potatoes, cut into chunks
- small pack coriander, chopped

FOR THE YELLOW RICE
- 50g/2oz butter
- 350g/12oz basmati rice
- 50g/2oz raisins
- 1 tsp golden caster sugar
- 1 tsp ground turmeric
- ¼ tsp ground white pepper
- 1 cinnamon stick, halved
- 8 cardamom pods, lightly crushed

1 Heat the slow cooker if necessary. Heat the oil in a large, wide pan. Add the onion and fry for 5 mins until softened, stirring every now and then. Stir in the garlic, ginger and cloves, and cook for 5 mins more, stirring frequently to stop it sticking. Add all the remaining spices and the fresh chilli, stir briefly, then tip in the tomatoes with 1½ cans of water, plus the chutney and crumbled stock cube.

2 Add the chicken thighs and potatoes, then tip into the slow cooker and cook on Low for 3 hours. Stir in the chopped coriander.

3 About 10 mins before you want to serve, make the rice. Put the butter, rice, raisins, sugar and spices in a large pan with 550ml/19fl oz water and ½ tsp salt. Bring to the boil and, when the butter has melted, stir, cover and cook for 10 mins. Turn off the heat and leave undisturbed for 5 mins. Fluff up and serve with the curry.

PER SERVING 605 kcals, fat 19g, saturates 7g, carbs 74g, sugars 13g, fibre 3g, protein 32g, salt 1.0g

Spicy African Chicken & Peanut Stew

This is lovely for fans of spicy food. Be wary of the Scotch bonnet chillies, though, as they're very hot!

 8–9 hours 4

- 150ml/¼ pint hot chicken stock
- 175g/6oz smooth peanut butter
- 1½ tbsp sunflower oil
- 1 onion, halved and thinly sliced
- 1½ tbsp finely chopped ginger
- ½ tsp cayenne (optional)
- 2 tsp each ground coriander and cumin
- 1 Scotch bonnet chilli, deseeded and chopped
- 1 bay leaf
- ½ x 400g can chopped tomatoes
- 800g pack chicken thighs and drumsticks, skin removed
- 2 small sweet potatoes, cut into big chunks
- 1 red pepper, deseeded and cut into chunks
- good handful coriander, roughly chopped
- rice, to serve (optional)
- lime wedges for squeezing over (optional)

1 Heat the slow cooker if necessary. In a jug, pour the hot stock over the peanut butter and stir until dissolved. Heat the oil in a frying pan and fry the onion, ginger, cayenne, if using, ½ teaspoon black pepper, the coriander, cumin, chilli and bay leaf until the onion is softened. Tip into the slow cooker pot.

2 Stir in the tomatoes and the peanut stock, then stir in the chicken pieces, sweet potatoes and pepper. Cover and cook on Low for 7–8 hours until the chicken is tender. Season to taste and stir in most of the chopped coriander.

3 Serve sprinkled with the reserved coriander, with some lime wedges for squeezing over and some rice, if you like.

PER SERVING 633 kcals, fat 40g, saturates 10g, carbs 25g, sugars 12g, fibre 4g, protein 44g, salt 0.8g

Jerk Pulled Pork with Banana Salsa

This is great party fodder and pretty much prepare-ahead – only the salsa needs to be made at the last minute.

 8-9 hours, plus overnight marinating · 6-8

- 100g/4oz sea salt
- 200g/8oz dark muscovado sugar
- 2kg/4lb 8oz piece boned shoulder of pork, trimmed of rind, but leave fat
- 4 tbsp jerk seasoning (we used Bart), mixed with 2 tsp ground cinnamon
- 500ml/18fl oz pineapple juice
- 50g/2oz black treacle
- 2 x 400g cans black beans, drained and rinsed well
- lots of soft flour tortillas (2-3 per person, depending on size and appetites)
- big pot of natural yogurt and shredded lettuce, to serve (optional)

FOR THE BANANA SALSA
- 3 firm bananas, diced
- 1 red onion, finely diced
- 2 just-ripe avocados
- juice 1 lemon
- juice 2 limes
- 1-2 red chillies, deseeded and diced
- small pack coriander, stalks finely chopped, leaves roughly chopped

1 The day before, mix the sea salt and 100g/4oz of the sugar in a large food bag. Add the pork and coat it well, then leave it in the fridge overnight.

2 The next day, remove the pork and wipe the meat down with kitchen paper to remove any excess sugar or salt, then rub 3 tablespoons of the jerk spices all over.

3 Heat the slow cooker if necessary. Mix together the remaining 100g/4oz sugar with 100ml/4fl oz of the pineapple juice, the remaining jerk spices and the treacle, and rub half over the pork. Pour the rest of the treacle mixture and pineapple juice into the slow cooker pot. Add the pork and cover with a sheet of baking parchment to seal in the steam. Put on the lid and cook on Low for 7-8 hours, turning the joint over halfway through the cooking time. Test the meat and it should be very tender and pull away in shreds.

4 If you want the outside of the meat to be charred, transfer the pork to a roasting tin and baste with the pot juices. Roast in the oven at 140C/120C fan/gas 1 for 1 hour. Rest the pork on a platter for 20 mins and pour any juices from the tin into a fat-separating jug.

5 To make the salsa, put the banana in a bowl with the onion. Stone, peel and dice the avocados and add these, too. Mix in the lemon and lime juice, chillies, coriander and some seasoning to taste.

6 Heat the black beans in a microwave, and warm the tortillas following pack instructions. Add a couple of forks next to the pork for shredding, discard the fat from the cooking juices, and serve the rest alongside for pouring. Serve the pork with the wraps, beans, banana salsa, yogurt and shredded lettuce, if you like.

PER SERVING (8) 822 kcals, fat 28g, saturates 9g, carbs 88g, sugars 34g, fibre 8g, protein 52g, salt 2.4g

Braised Pork with Plums

Pork shoulder is the perfect cut of meat for the slow cooker as it really needs long, slow braising to become lovely and tender.

🕐 9-11 hours, plus marinating   8

- about 1.6kg/3lb 8oz pork shoulder, cut into very large chunks
- 5 tbsp each rice wine and soy sauce
- generous thumb-sized piece ginger
- 5 garlic cloves
- 1 red chilli, deseeded and finely chopped
- 2 tbsp vegetable oil
- bunch spring onions, finely sliced
- 1 cinnamon stick
- 2 star anise
- 2 tsp Chinese five-spice powder
- 2 tbsp each sugar (any type) and tomato purée
- 500ml/18fl oz chicken stock
- 6 ripe plums, halved and stoned

1 Mix the pork with the rice wine and soy, plus half of the ginger, garlic and chilli. Marinate for 1–24 hours.
2 Heat the slow cooker if necessary. Heat the oil in a large pan. Tip in half the spring onions, the remaining ginger, garlic and chilli, and the cinnamon, star anise, five-spice, sugar and purée. Fry until soft, then lift the pork from the marinade and add to the pan, frying until the meat is sealed but not browned. Tip everything into the slow cooker pot with the marinade and stock. Cover and cook for 8–9 hours on Low.
3 Skim any fat off the surface halfway through cooking, if you can. Stir in the plums an hour before the end of the cooking time.
4 Scoop the meat and plums from the pot. Tip the rest of the slow cooker contents into a large pan and boil for 5–10 mins until the sauce is slightly syrupy. Return the pork and plums to gently warm through, then scatter with the remaining spring onions to serve.

PER SERVING 530 kcals, fat 36g, saturates 13g, carbs 11g, sugars 10g, fibre 1g, protein 40g, salt 2.87g

Sweet & Sour Chicken Adobo

· ·

This dish is based on a classic Filipino stew, made with lots of vinegar and sweetened with sugar. The sauce cooks down until rich and glossy and is perfect served with stir-fried veg.

 6-7 hours 4

- 4 tbsp vegetable oil
- 600g/1lb 5oz boneless chicken thighs, skin removed, cut in half
- 2 tbsp cornflour, plus 1-2 tsp extra (optional)
- 1 large onion, cut into chunky pieces
- 5 garlic cloves, crushed
- 2 red peppers, deseeded and cut into chunky pieces
- 400ml can coconut milk
- 100ml/3½fl oz low-salt soy sauce
- 100ml/3½fl oz white wine vinegar
- 50g/2oz light brown soft sugar
- 6 bay leaves
- basmati or brown rice, to serve

1 Heat the slow cooker if necessary. Heat half the oil in a large pan. Put the chicken in a large bowl, season well and toss through the cornflour, then cook in batches until browned all over (don't overcrowd the pan or the chicken won't brown). Tip each batch straight into the slow cooker as you go, adding a little more oil to the pan if you need to. Add the onion, garlic and peppers, cook for a few mins to just soften, then add these to the slow cooker too.

2 If there is any cornflour remaining in the bowl, add a drop of the coconut milk and swirl it around, then pour into the slow cooker. Add the remaining coconut milk, the soy sauce, vinegar, sugar and bay leaves and season with plenty of black pepper. Cover with the lid and cook on Low for 5-6 hours until the meat is tender and the sauce has thickened. If the sauce in the slow cooker is too thin, thicken it with the remaining cornflour.

3 Mix 1-2 tsp cornflour with 1-2 tsp cold water to make a paste. Ladle two or three spoonfuls of the sauce into a saucepan and bring to a simmer, then stir in the cornflour paste and cook for 1-2 mins to thicken. Stir back into the slow cooker and cook on High for 10 mins more. Serve with rice and stir-fried veg.

· ·

PER SERVING 644 kcals, fat 34g, saturates 17g, carbs 46g, sugars 25g, fibre 3g, protein 37g, salt 3.4g

Sticky Pork & Pineapple Hotpot

If you loved sweet & sour pork stews from the past here's an updated version with a little bit of Thai and Vietnamese influence.

 5 hours 8

- 1 tbsp vegetable oil
- 1.5kg/3lb 5oz (about 8) pork shoulder steaks, each cut into 4 thick strips
- 3 onions, roughly chopped
- 4 garlic cloves, thinly sliced
- small bunch coriander, stalks finely chopped, leaves reserved
- 3 Thai red chillies, 2 sliced, 1 left whole and pricked
- 3 star anise
- 100g/4oz dark soft brown sugar
- 2 tbsp tomato purée
- 2 tbsp fish sauce
- 600ml/1 pint chicken stock
- 350g/12oz fresh pineapple, cut into chunks

1 Heat the slow cooker if necessary. Heat the oil in a large, flameproof casserole dish. Season the pork and brown it in two or three batches until golden, about 5 mins per batch. Set aside in a bowl. Stir the onions into the remaining fat, cover and soften for 5 mins – they will take on the browned colour of the meat.

2 Add the garlic, coriander stalks, chillies and anise to the dish, sizzle for 1 min, stirring often, then mix in the sugar and tomato purée. When these have melted and it looks a bit like barbecue sauce, return the pork and its resting juices to the dish, along with the fish sauce, stock and the pineapple chunks.

3 Tip into the slow cooker pot, cover and cook on Low for 4 hours. The pork will be meltingly soft when ready. If the sauce is thin, lift the pork into a warmed serving dish, skin off any fat, then tip the juice into a pan and simmer on the hob until the sauce has slightly thickened. Leave to cool for 5 mins, taste for seasoning, pour over the pork and sprinkle over the coriander leaves.

PER SERVING 339 kcals, fat 10g, saturates 3g, carbs 21g, sugars 19g, fibre 2g, protein 40g, salt 1.1g

Red Thai Salmon Curry

You can easily experiment with this curry to suit your mood. Swap the Thai red curry paste for green or yellow, and the salmon for white fish or prawns.

 2-2½ hours 4

- 1 tsp vegetable or sunflower oil
- 1 tbsp Thai red curry paste
- 1 onion, sliced
- 250ml/9fl oz reduced-fat coconut milk
- 2 x 250g skinless salmon fillets, cut into chunks
- 200g/7oz trimmed green beans
- plain rice, to serve

1 Heat the slow cooker if necessary. Heat the oil in a large pan, then add the curry paste. Stir in the onion, then cook gently for about 5 mins until softened.
2 Transfer to the slow cooker pot with the coconut milk, salmon chunks and beans. Cook on Low for 1½–2 hours until the fish flakes easily and the beans are cooked but have a little crunch. Serve with plain rice.

PER SERVING 326 kcals, fat 22g, saturates 9g, carbs 5g, sugars 4g, fibre 22g, protein 27g, salt 0.46g

Thai Beef Curry

You can use a shop-bought paste for this curry, but this authentic Thai one really is worth the effort. This is good served with sticky Thai rice and wilted greens.

 8½ hours 8

- 2-3 tbsp sunflower oil
- 2kg/4lb 8oz beef short ribs (bone-in ribs left whole) or brisket, cut into large chunks
- large bunch coriander
- 2 lemongrass stalks, 1 bashed, 1 roughly chopped
- 3 garlic cloves, chopped
- 1-2 green chillies, roughly chopped, deseeded if you like
- 2cm/¾in-piece galangal or ginger, peeled and chopped
- 50ml/2fl oz rice wine vinegar
- 50ml/2fl oz fish sauce
- 2 tbsp light brown sugar
- 400g can coconut milk
- 2 star anise
- 6 kaffir lime leaves
- juice 2 limes, plus wedges to serve

1 Heat a little of the oil in a large pan and brown the beef in batches, removing to a plate and reserving any juices. Meanwhile, in a mini chopper or food processor, whizz half the coriander, the chopped lemongrass, garlic, chillies and galangal with the rest of the oil until you have a rough paste.

2 Heat the slow cooker if necessary. Fry the paste for a few mins, then add the beef and all the remaining ingredients, apart from the remaining coriander and lime juice. Tip into the slow cooker, cover and cook on Low for 8 hours, or until the meat is falling off the bone.

3 If using beef ribs, remove the bones from the beef, then shred the meat with two forks. If the sauce is too thin, strain it off and boil it to reduce. Stir in the remaining coriander and lime juice, then season with more fish sauce or sugar.

PER SERVING 541 kcals, fat 40g, saturates 20g, carbs 10g, sugars 7g, fibre none, protein 34g, salt 1.5g

Slow-cooked Beetroot & Beef Curry

You don't often think beetroot and curry, but the earthy flavours work really well with the spices.

🕐 4-4½ hours   🍽 3-4

- 3-4 tbsp sunflower oil
- 3 green cardamoms
- 2.5cm/1in piece of cinnamon
- 1 tsp each cumin and coriander seeds
- 2 medium red onions, sliced
- 1 tsp each grated garlic and ginger
- 2 medium tomatoes, chopped
- 1 tsp red chilli powder
- 450g/1lb stewing beef, cut into 2.5cm/1in chunks
- 350g/12oz raw beetroot, grated

TO SERVE
- small pack coriander leaves
- 1 green chilli, chopped
- squeeze of ½ lime
- naan bread or basmati rice

1 Heat the slow cooker if necessary. Using a large, non-stick wok or saucepan, heat the oil over a medium flame, add the cardamom, cinnamon, cumin and coriander seeds. Once the spices start to sizzle, add the onions and stir-fry until light golden brown.

2 Add the garlic and ginger and cook for 1 min. Add a splash of water if the garlic and ginger start to stick to the pan, then add the tomatoes and cook until soft.

3 Add 1 tsp salt, chilli powder and the beef, turn up the heat and stir-fry until the meat is sealed on all sides. Stir in the beetroot and 75ml/3fl oz water then tip into the slow cooker pot, cover and cook on Low for 3½ – 4 hours until the beef is tender

4 The finished dish should be a thick, mushy curry with chunky, tender beef pieces and softened beetroot. Sprinkle with the coriander leaves and green chilli; add a squeeze of lime, and serve with naan or basmati rice.

PER SERVING (3) 326 kcals, fat 20g, saturates 5g, carbs 12g, sugars 10g, fibre 4g, protein 25g, salt 1.5g

Light Chicken Korma

This curry is low-fat and low-calorie, so there's no excuse not to make it right away and tuck in!

 3 hours 4

- 1 onion, chopped
- 2 garlic cloves, roughly chopped
- thumb-sized piece ginger, roughly chopped
- 4 tbsp korma paste
- 50g/2oz ground almonds
- 4 tbsp sultanas
- 250ml/9fl oz chicken stock
- ¼ tsp golden caster sugar
- 4 boneless chicken breasts, skin removed
- 150g pot fat-free Greek yogurt
- small bunch coriander, chopped
- few flaked almonds, to scatter (optional)
- basmati rice, to serve

1 Heat the slow cooker if necessary. Put the onion, garlic and ginger in a food processor and whizz to a paste. Scrape the paste into the slow cooker pot and mix with the korma paste, ground almonds, sultanas, chicken stock and sugar. Push in the chicken breasts, cover and cook on High for 2 hours until the chicken is cooked through and tender.

2 Fish out the chicken breasts and dice into chunks. Stir back into the sauce. Cover and cook for 20–30 mins more on High, just to heat through.

3 Remove from the heat, stir in the yogurt and some seasoning, then scatter over the coriander and flaked almonds, if using. Serve with brown or white basmati rice.

PER SERVING 376 kcals, fat 11g, saturates 1g, carbs 28g, sugars 26g, fibre 3g, protein 40g, salt 1.1g

Winter Vegetable Curry with Mango Raita

Use your favourite blend of curry paste in this depending how spicy you like your curries.

 4-4½ hours 4

- 2 tbsp vegetable oil
- 2 onions, thinly sliced
- ½ medium butternut squash, peeled, deseeded and cut into cubes
- 4 carrots, cut into batons
- 2 parsnips, cut into batons
- 3-4 tbsp curry paste
- 8 large ripe tomatoes, cut into wedges
- 6 garlic cloves, peeled
- thumb-sized piece ginger, peeled and chopped
- small pack coriander, chopped
- small pack toasted flaked almonds

FOR THE RAITA
- 6 tbsp low-fat natural yogurt
- 100g/4oz mango, cut into cubes
- 1 tbsp mango chutney

1 Heat the slow cooker if necessary. Heat the oil in a large pan. Tip in the onions and cook for 10 mins until soft. Stir in the squash, carrots and parsnips, and cook for 5 mins until they begin to soften. Add the curry paste and cook for another 3 mins.

2 Whizz six of the tomatoes, the garlic and ginger in a food processor until smooth, then pour over the vegetables with 200ml/7fl oz water. Tip the mixture into the slow cooker pot, cover and cook on High for 3 hours. Add the remaining tomatoes and most of the coriander and cook for 30 mins–1 hour more until the vegetables are tender.

3 Meanwhile, mix the yogurt, mango and chutney in a small bowl. Scatter the curry with remaining coriander and the almonds and serve with rice and the raita.

PER SERVING 467 kcals, fat 13g, saturates 2g, carbs 73g, sugars 31g, fibre 12g, protein 13g, salt 0.8g

Cauliflower & Tomato Curry

Green chillies and tamarind spark up this vegetarian curry. If making this midweek, use curry pastes and spice mixtures, like garam masala, instead of the individual spices.

 3-3½ hours 4

- 2 onions, 1 quartered, the other thinly sliced
- 5cm/2in piece ginger, peeled and sliced
- 2 green chillies, 1 halved and deseeded, the other sliced
- 3 garlic cloves, chopped
- 2 tbsp vegetable oil
- ½ tsp turmeric
- 2 tsp black or yellow mustard seeds
- 1 tsp each cumin, coriander and fennel seeds
- 10 curry leaves
- 3 tbsp tamarind purée (we used Bart)
- 400ml/14fl oz passata
- 200ml/7fl oz vegetable stock
- 3 tbsp desiccated coconut
- 1 cauliflower, cut into medium florets
- small handful coriander leaves, chopped
- basmati rice, to serve
- lime pickle and mango chutney, to serve (optional)

1 Heat the slow cooker if necessary. In a blender or food processor, purée the quartered onion, ginger, halved green chilli and garlic to make a paste. Add a dash of water if you need to help it on its way.

2 In a large saucepan, heat the oil. Add the sliced onion and paste and season well, then fry for 10-12 mins until golden. Add all the spices and curry leaves and cook a few mins more.

3 Stir in the tamarind, passata, stock, coconut and cauliflower and bring to the boil. Tip into the slow cooker pot. Cover and cook on High for 2½–3 hours depending how soft you want the cauliflower to be. Serve with rice, coriander leaves, the remaining sliced green chilli and lime pickle and mango chutney, if you like.

PER SERVING 307 kcals, fat 15g, saturates 7g, carbs 30g, sugars 27g, fibre 8g, protein 9g, salt 0.2g

Goan Prawn & Coconut Curry with Cumin Rice

Making an authentic-tasting curry from scratch doesn't have to take a lot of effort.

 4–5 hours 2

- 1 tbsp sunflower oil
- 1 onion, thinly sliced
- 1 tbsp grated ginger
- 2 garlic cloves, crushed
- 1 red chilli, deseeded and sliced
- ½ tsp each turmeric and chilli powder
- 1 tsp ground coriander
- 10 curry leaves
- 1 large potato, diced
- 300ml/½ pint half-fat coconut milk
- 8 cherry tomatoes, halved
- handful baby leaf spinach
- 200g pack raw peeled prawns

FOR THE CUMIN RICE
- 1 tsp cumin seeds
- 175g/6oz basmati rice

1 Heat the slow cooker if necessary. Heat the oil in a frying pan and fry the onion, ginger, garlic and chilli for 5 mins until starting to soften. Scrape into the slow cooker with the spices, curry leaves, potato, coconut milk and tomatoes. Cover and cook for 3 hours on High until the potato is tender.

2 Add the spinach and prawns. Cook for 30 mins–1 hour more until the prawns are cooked.

3 Meanwhile, make the rice. Tip the cumin seeds into a pan and toast over a dry heat for 30 seconds. Add the rice, salt to taste and 400ml/14fl oz water, then cover and cook for 8–10 mins until the rice is tender and the water has been absorbed. Serve with the curry.

PER SERVING 771 kcals, fat 22g, saturates 13g, carbs 105g, sugars 9g, fibre 6g, protein 33g, salt 0.6g

Chapter 4:

EASY ENTERTAINING

Andalusian-style Chicken

Spicy, sweet and fragrant, this is bursting with Moorish flavours. Serve with crusty bread or rice.

 5½ hours   6

- generous pinch of saffron
- 1 chicken stock cube, crumbled into 300ml/ ½ pint boiling water
- 2 tbsp olive oil
- 2 small onions, thinly sliced
- 12 bone-in chicken thighs, skin removed
- ¼ tsp ground cinnamon
- 1-2 red chillies, deseeded and chopped
- 4 tbsp Sherry vinegar
- 1-2 tbsp clear honey
- 12 cherry tomatoes, quartered
- 2 tbsp raisins
- handful of coriander, roughly chopped, to garnish
- 50g/2oz toasted pine nuts or almonds, to garnish

1 Heat the slow cooker if necessary. Stir the saffron into the hot stock to infuse. Heat the oil in a pan and fry the onions until soft and just beginning to turn golden. Tip into the slow cooker pot. Add the chicken to the pan and fry for a few mins until the chicken is browned all over, then add that to the pot too.

2 Stir the cinnamon and chilli into the pan, then add the stock, vinegar, honey, tomatoes and raisins and bring to the boil. Tip into the slow cooker, cover and cook on Low for 5 hours until the chicken is tender. Check the sauce and if it is a little thin, pour it from the pot and boil rapidly in a frying pan to reduce it. Pour back into the pot, scatter with the coriander and nuts, and serve.

PER SERVING 236 kcals, fat 11g, saturates 1g, carbs 11g, sugars 10g, fibre 1g, protein 23g, salt 0.5g

Chicken with Sweet Wine & Garlic

This is a classic French dish, delicious served with buttered boiled potatoes and green vegetables.

 9 hours 4

- 2 tbsp seasoned flour
- 1.5kg/3lb 5oz whole chicken, jointed into 8 pieces
- 2–4 tbsp olive oil
- 2 shallots, finely chopped
- 100ml/4fl oz sweet wine, such as Sauternes
- 200ml/7fl oz chicken stock
- sprig each parsley, thyme and bay tied with string
- 1 garlic bulb
- 50g/2oz butter
- 200g/7oz chestnut mushrooms
- 3 rounded tbsp crème fraîche
- a little lemon juice, if needed

1 Heat the slow cooker if necessary. Tip the flour into a large food bag. Add the chicken pieces, two at a time, and shake well to coat evenly. Heat 2 tablespoons of the oil in a large pan, add a few pieces of the chicken and fry on all sides until well browned – repeat in batches. Remove the browned chicken to your slow cooker pot.

2 Add the shallots, wine, stock, herbs, garlic and seasoning, cover and cook for 8 hours on Low.

3 Remove the garlic and peel the cloves. Heat half the butter and a splash of the oil in a frying pan. Add the mushrooms and fry over a moderate heat until cooked. Stir into the chicken. Wipe out the pan and add the remaining butter and another splash of the oil. Add the garlic cloves and fry gently, until lightly browned. Stir in the crème fraîche, a squeeze of lemon juice and seasoning.

4 To serve, spoon the chicken and sauce on to a platter and scatter with the garlic.

PER SERVING 828 kcals, fat 62g, saturates 22g, carbs 9g, sugars 4g, fibre 1g, protein 51g, salt 0.81g

Beef & Stout Stew with Carrots

Sweet slow-cooked melty carrots are one of the best bits of a rustic stew. This stew can be frozen for up to 3 months, then simply defrosted then reheated until piping hot.

 8½–9½ hours   4

- 2 tbsp vegetable oil
- 1kg/2lb 4oz stewing beef, cut into large chunks
- 2 tbsp plain flour
- 1 onion, roughly chopped
- 10 carrots, cut into large chunks
- 400ml/14fl oz Guinness or other stout
- 1 beef stock cube
- pinch sugar
- 3 bay leaves
- big thyme sprig

1. Heat the slow cooker if necessary. Heat the oil in a large frying pan and brown the meat really well in batches, then transfer to the slow cooker pot. Stir in the flour until it disappears. Add the onion, carrots and stout and crumble in the stock cube. Season the stew with some salt and pepper and the sugar. Tuck in the herbs.
2. Cover and cook on Low for 8–9 hours until the beef is really tender.

PER SERVING 562 kcals, fat 23g, saturates 8g, carbs 26g, sugars 20g, fibre 6g, protein 58g, salt 1.5g

Pork & Beef Chilli with Lemon & Pancetta

This is the chilli equivalent of making a rich ragu rather than a quicker mince Bolognese –
each has its place, but this is a little more special for entertaining friends.

 7 hours   6

- 75g/2½oz diced pancetta
- 2-3 tbsp olive oil
- 2 onions, chopped
- 4 garlic cloves, finely chopped
- 500g/1lb 2oz lean belly pork slices, cut into small chunks
- 700g/1lb 9oz skirt steak or lean stewing beef, cut into small chunks
- 3 tbsp smoked sweet paprika or chilli powder
- 1 tsp ground cumin
- 1 tbsp plain flour
- 2 bay leaves
- 1 lemon, quartered lengthways, pithy core and seeds removed then chopped into small pieces
- 2 tsp dried oregano
- 2 tbsp tomato purée
- 300ml/½ pint red wine
- 300ml/½ pint chicken or beef stock
- 400g can black beans, drained and rinsed

TO SERVE
- rice or couscous
- 300ml/½ pint soured cream
- 4 small firm ripe avocados, chopped
- juice 2 limes, plus extra wedges to serve (optional)
- sweet chilli dipping sauce, to serve
- chopped coriander or chives, to serve

1 Heat the slow cooker if necessary. In a large pan, fry the pancetta in 1 tablespoon oil over a medium heat until it is crisp and the fat has melted. Stir in the onions and garlic and cook, stirring often, for 10 mins until soft. Tip into the slow cooker pot.
2 Return the pan to the heat with some more oil and brown the pork and beef in batches until brown. Add to the softened onions.
3 Stir the sweet paprika and cumin into the pan juices with the flour, and cook briefly over a low heat, stirring constantly. Add the bay leaves, ½ tsp salt, the lemon, oregano, tomato purée, red wine and stock. Bring to a simmer, stirring often, then pour in to the pot and stir well. Cook on Low for 6 hours until the meat is tender.
4 Add the beans to the chilli and leave to heat briefly. Serve with rice or couscous, a dollop of soured cream, slices of avocado tossed in lime juice, a splash of chilli sauce, sprinkling of coriander or chives, and lime wedges, if you like.

PER SERVING 555 kcals, fat 29g, saturates 9g, carbs 12g, sugars 4g, fibre 4g, protein 51g, salt 1.9g

BBQ Pulled Pork

If you love to barbecue in the summer use your slow cooker to cook a piece of pork long and slow, then finish it off over the coals. Serve it in chunks of French bread with coleslaw.

 9 hours 8

- 1 tbsp sunflower oil
- 2 onions, sliced
- 3 bay leaves
- 1 tbsp each mustard powder and smoked paprika
- 1½-2kg/3lb 5oz-4lb 8oz pork shoulder, boned with rind attached and tied
- 140g/5oz tomato ketchup
- 4 tbsp red wine vinegar
- 1 tbsp Worcestershire sauce
- 3 tbsp soft dark brown sugar
- 2 French sticks, sliced into rolls, and coleslaw, to serve

1 Heat the slow cooker if necessary. Heat the oil in a large frying pan and fry the onions with the bay leaves for 10 mins until softened and starting to colour. Tip into the slow cooker pot (it needs to be a large one).

2 Mix the mustard powder, paprika and 1 tsp ground black pepper with a good pinch of salt. Rub this all over the pork, making sure you rub it into all the crevices. Place the pork on top of the onions and pour in 300ml/½ pint water. Cover and cook on Low for 8 hours quickly turning the meat over halfway through. Chill until ready to barbecue.

3 Light the barbecue. Remove the pork from the pot and pat dry. Place the onions and liquid in a large frying pan, add the ketchup, vinegar, Worcestershire sauce and brown sugar and bubble vigorously for 10–15 mins until thick and glossy. Remove the bay leaves and pour the sauce into a food processor; blitz until smooth. Smear half the sauce mixture over the meat.

4 Once the barbecue flames have died down, put on the pork, skin-side down. Cook for 15 mins until nicely charred, then turn over and cook for another 10 mins. The meat will be very tender, so be careful not to lose any between the bars. The coals might flare as the sauce drips on to it, so you can cook on a sheet of foil if you prefer.

5 Lift the pork onto a large plate or tray and peel off the skin. Using two forks, shred the meat into chunky pieces. Add 3-4 tablespoons of the barbecue sauce to the meat and toss everything well to coat. Pile into rolls and serve with extra sauce and a little coleslaw.

PER SERVING 520 kcals, fat 29g, saturates 10g, carbs 15g, sugars 14g, fibre 1g, protein 49g, salt 1.1g

Braised Ox Cheek Wellingtons with Peppercorn Gravy

This uses slow-cooked ox cheek cooked with dried mushrooms instead of the usual steak. It is perfect for spoiling someone special. Serve with green vegetables.

 8 hours, plus chilling  2 easily doubled

- 1 ox cheek, about 350g/12oz, trimmed of any sinew and cut into 4 chunks
- 1 tbsp plain flour, plus a little for dusting
- 1 tsp English mustard powder
- 1 tbsp sunflower oil
- 1 small red onion, roughly chopped
- 3 thyme sprigs
- 1 beef stock cube
- 2 tbsp dried porcini mushrooms
- knob of butter
- 1 garlic clove, crushed
- 100g/4oz chestnut mushrooms, finely chopped
- 500g ready-made puff pastry
- 4 slices prosciutto
- 1 egg, beaten
- 100ml/3½fl oz double cream
- 1 tsp black peppercorns, crushed using a pestle and mortar

1 Heat the slow cooker if necessary. Toss the ox cheek in the flour and mustard, then brown in the oil in a frying pan. Add the onion and cook until soft and just caramelising. Add the thyme, stock cube, porcini and seasoning. Pour in 600ml/1 pint water and bring to the boil. Tip into the slow cooker, cover and cook on Low for 6 hours until really tender. Strain the juice and boil to reduce by two-thirds.

2 Meanwhile, melt the butter in a pan. Add the garlic, stir for 1 min but don't brown, then add the mushrooms and cook for 10–12 mins until the pan is dry and the mushrooms are golden. Season and set aside.

3 Shred the ox cheek and add 3-4 tablespoons of the liquid back to the meat, along with the cooked mushrooms. Chill (with the remaining liquid) for 3 hours, or overnight.

4 Roll out the pastry on a floured surface to the thickness of a £1 coin. Cut out 2 x 12cm/5in circles and 2 x 15cm/6in circles using two plates. Arrange the prosciutto in pairs on top of the smaller circles in a cross shape. Split the meat mixture in half and mound each portion on top of the prosciutto. Fold the prosciutto over the meat to encase it, then flip the parcel over, so the smooth side is facing up on top of the pastry. Brush the edge of each circle with egg, then place the larger circles on top. Use your hands to create a domed centre, then crimp the edges with a fork or your fingers to seal in the meat. Score the pastry in a criss-cross pattern and brush over with egg.

5 Use any pastry scraps to cut out a heart or leaves for each pie, stick on top and brush with egg. Poke a steam hole on either side of each heart. Place each Wellington on a square of baking parchment and chill for at least 30 mins.

6 Heat oven to 200C/180C fan/gas 6 and put a baking tray in the oven to heat up. Slide the Wellingtons on their parchment onto the hot tray and bake for 30 mins. Meanwhile, reheat the cooking liquid, add the cream and peppercorns and serve warm with the Wellingtons.

PER SERVING 1,446 kcals, fat 94g, saturates 45g, carbs 90g, sugars 5g, fibre 2g, protein 58g, salt 4.9g

Chinese-braised Beef with Ginger

You can't go wrong with this dish – it has such a depth of flavour. Serve it with some jasmine rice and a few stir-fried Chinese greens.

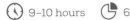 9-10 hours   6

- 3–4 tbsp sunflower or vegetable oil
- 1.25kg/2lb 12oz stewing beef, cut into very large chunks
- 2 onions
- 50g/2oz piece ginger
- 3 garlic cloves
- small bunch coriander, leaves and stalks separated
- 2 tsp Chinese five-spice powder
- 6 star anise
- 1 tsp black peppercorns
- 100g/4oz dark brown muscovado sugar
- 50ml/2fl oz dark soy sauce
- 50ml/2fl oz light soy sauce
- 2 tbsp tomato purée
- 500ml/18fl oz beef stock
- thumb-sized chunk ginger, shredded into matchsticks

1 Heat the slow cooker if necessary. Heat a little of the oil in a large frying pan. Add the beef chunks, in batches, and fry until browned, then transfer the beef to the slow cooker. Roughly chop the onions, ginger, garlic and coriander stalks. Put in a food processor and whizz to a paste.

2 Wipe any oil out of the pan in which you browned the beef. Add the paste with a splash of water and gently fry until the paste is fragrant and softened (add more water if the paste sticks). Add to the slow cooker pot with the five-spice, star anise, peppercorns, sugar, soy sauces, tomato purée and stock. Cover and cook on Low for 8–9 hours until the beef is tender.

3 Lift the beef out of the slow cooker and set aside. Tip the sauce into a big pan and boil until reduced by about half and thickened. Meanwhile, fry the ginger matchsticks in the remaining oil until golden and crispy. Return the beef to the sauce and scatter with the ginger.

PER SERVING 405 kcals, fat 11g, saturates 4g, carbs 26g, sugars 23g, fibre 1g, protein 51g, salt 3.96g

Turkish Lamb Pilaf

This is a complete meal in one, with no need for any extra accompaniments, so spoon straight from the pot and tuck in for a casual night in with friends!

🕐 3½–4½ hours   🥘 4

- 1 tbsp olive oil
- 2 cinnamon sticks, broken in half
- 1 tsp each ground cumin, coriander and turmeric
- 1 large onion, halved and sliced
- 500g/1lb 2oz lean lamb neck fillet, cubed
- 250g/9oz basmati rice
- 1 lamb or vegetable stock cube
- 12 ready-to-eat dried apricots
- small handful toasted pine nuts or toasted flaked almonds, to garnish
- handful mint leaves, roughly chopped, to garnish

1 Heat the slow cooker if necessary, then heat the oil in a frying pan. Fry the cinnamon, spices and onion together for 5–10 mins until starting to turn golden. Turn up the heat, stir in the lamb, and fry until the meat changes colour. Tip into the slow cooker pot with the rice and stir to mix.

2 Pour in 500ml/18fl oz boiling water, crumble in the stock cube, add the apricots, then season to taste. Cook on Low for 3–4 hours until the rice is tender and the stock has been absorbed. Toss in the pine nuts or almonds and the mint, and serve.

PER SERVING 584 kcals, fat 24g, saturates 9g, carbs 65g, sugars none, fibre 1g, protein 32g, salt 1.4g

Shepherd's Pie with Lamb's Liver

Slow cooking the mince with lamb's liver packs this classic dish with loads of flavour. To save time, chop the liver then the vegetables in a food processor.

 5½-6½ hours 4-6

- 2 tbsp olive oil
- 500g/1lb 2oz lamb mince
- 250g/9oz prepared lamb's liver (or chicken livers), finely chopped
- 250ml/9fl oz chicken or lamb stock
- 2 onions, finely chopped
- 2 carrots, finely chopped
- 2 celery sticks, finely chopped
- few thyme sprigs
- 1 bay leaf
- 3 tbsp tomato purée
- 2 tbsp Worcestershire sauce, plus extra to serve
- seasonal vegetables, to serve

FOR THE MASH TOPPING
- 1.25kg/2lb 12oz Maris Piper potatoes, cut into large chunks
- 150-200ml/5-7fl oz milk
- 50g/2oz butter
- 50g/2oz mature Red Leicester or cheddar, grated
- 20g pack parsley, finely chopped

1 Heat the slow cooker if necessary. Heat 1 tablespoon oil in a large frying pan and fry the mince for 10 mins or until well browned. Add the liver and cook for a few mins until it changes colour. Tip the mince and liver into the slow cooker pot, deglaze the pan using a splash of the stock, then pour the liquid on top of the mince and liver mixture. Wipe out the pan.

2 Heat the rest of the oil. Add the vegetables and herbs, season and soften for 10 mins. Stir in the purée, Worcestershire sauce and remaining stock and bring to the boil. Pour into the slow cooker and stir well. Cover and cook on Low for 4–5 hours until tender. If any bits of liver look prominent, mash them into the sauce.

3 Start the potato topping with 30 mins cooking time to go. Heat oven to 190C/170C fan/gas 5. Boil the potatoes until tender, then drain. Warm 150ml/5fl oz of milk in the potato pan, then add the drained potatoes and the butter. Mash until smooth, adding more milk if needed. Season generously and stir through most of the cheese and all the parsley.

4 When the mince and liver is ready, transfer it to a deep baking dish. Top with the mash, smoothing it to the edges of the dish, then scallop the top with a knife or leave it rough. Scatter with the rest of the cheese and bake for 45 mins until golden and bubbling. Let it stand for 5 mins, then serve with seasonal vegetables and an extra dash of Worcestershire sauce.

PER SERVING (6) 593 kcals, fat 28g, saturates 13g, carbs 43g, sugars 9g, fibre 6g, protein 38g, salt 0.8g

Braised Shoulder of Lamb with Jewelled Stuffing

You can stuff and assemble the lamb the night before, chill it overnight, then start cooking at breakfast. By the evening your dinner will be meltingly tender.

 11½–13½ hours   6

- 1.5kg/3lb 5oz boned shoulder of lamb
- 2 tbsp sunflower oil
- 1 onion, roughly chopped
- 75ml/2½fl oz white wine
- 350ml/12fl oz chicken stock
- strip orange zest
- 1 cinnamon stick
- 2 bay leaves
- small pack parsley, to garnish

FOR THE STUFFING
- 50g/2oz each stoned dates and ready-to-eat dried apricots, roughly chopped
- 25g/1oz each dried cranberries and shelled pistachio nuts, chopped
- handful parsley, finely chopped, plus extra for sprinkling
- 1 shallot, finely chopped
- zest ½ orange
- 3 slices stale bread, whizzed into crumbs

1 To make the stuffing, soak the dates, apricots and cranberries in boiling water for 30 mins, then drain and squeeze dry. Mix with the rest of the stuffing ingredients and some seasoning.

2 Unroll the lamb and season it well on both sides. Spread the stuffing over one side, then roll up the meat and secure it with string. Heat the oil in a large frying pan, add the lamb and brown it well.

3 Heat the slow cooker if necessary. Put in the onion, wine, stock, orange zest, cinnamon and bay leaves, then sit in the lamb. Cover and cook on Low for 10–12 hours until the meat is really tender. Remove and wrap with foil.

4 Strain the remaining juices and spoon off any surface fat, then put the juices into a wide pan and boil to reduce for 5–10 mins, until slightly thickened. Season. Slice the lamb and serve with the sauce and parsley sprinkled over.

PER SERVING 767 kcals, fat 52g, saturates 24g, carbs 25g, sugars 15g, fibre 2g, protein 50g, salt 0.81g

Sweet Pork Belly with Vietnamese-style Salad & Smashed Peanuts

You can marinate the pork in the sauce overnight if you want to get ahead with the preparation. Serve with coconut rice.

 4 hours   2   Easily doubled

- ½ tbsp sunflower oil
- 600g/1lb 5oz rindless belly pork rashers
- coconut rice, to serve (optional)

FOR THE SAUCE
- 6 tbsp hoisin sauce
- 3 tbsp clear honey
- 3 tbsp rice vinegar
- 3 tbsp soy sauce
- 4 tbsp tomato ketchup
- 2.5cm/1in piece ginger, peeled and finely chopped

FOR THE SALAD
- ¼ cucumber, cut in ribbons using a vegetable peeler
- 6 radishes, sliced
- 75g/2½oz sugar snap peas, halved horizontally
- 2 spring onions, thinly sliced
- 2 tbsp mint leaves, large leaves torn
- 2 tbsp Thai basil, large leaves torn (use coriander if you can't find this)
- 1 tbsp salted peanuts, toasted and lightly smashed in a pestle and mortar

FOR THE DRESSING
- 1 small red chilli, finely chopped
- ½ garlic clove, grated
- juice ½ lime
- ½ tsp light brown sugar
- 1 tbsp rice vinegar

1 Heat the slow cooker to High and add all of the sauce ingredients with 50ml/2fl oz water, then stir well. Heat the oil in a large frying pan and seal the pork on both sides. Add to the slow cooker pot and turn the rashers over in the sauce to coat them. Turn the dial to Low and cook for 3 hours until tender.

2 Meanwhile, prepare the salad. Toss all the ingredients, except the peanuts, together in a bowl. To make the dressing, combine all the ingredients and set aside.

3 When the pork is ready, tip the sauce from the pot into a small pan. Bring the sauce to the boil and let it bubble until thick and syrupy.

4 Toss the dressing through the salad and divide between two plates, then top with the smashed peanuts. Arrange the pork alongside the salad, then drizzle over the sauce. Serve with coconut rice, if you like.

PER SERVING 803 kcals, fat 37g, saturates 12g, carbs 58g, sugars 50g, fibre 4g, protein 58g, salt 7.7g

Normandy Pork with Apples & Cider

Inexpensive packs of pork shoulder steaks work well in this dish – or, if you can find them, pork cheeks will add a rich, gelatinous texture.

 7½–9½ hours 4

- 2 tbsp rapeseed or olive oil
- 600g/1lb 5oz pork shoulder or pork cheeks, fat and sinew trimmed, cut into chunky pieces
- 1 large onion, chopped
- 2 carrots, cut into chunky pieces
- 2 celery sticks, cut into chunky pieces
- 200g pack smoked bacon lardons
- 250ml/9fl oz dry cider
- 2 eating apples (we used Braeburn), cored and cut into chunky pieces
- 1 chicken stock cube
- 1 bay leaf
- 4 thyme sprigs, plus extra to serve (optional)
- 140g/5oz crème fraîche
- 1-2 tbsp Dijon mustard, plus extra to serve (optional)
- 1-2 tsp cornflour (optional)
- mashed potatoes and greens, to serve

1 Heat half the oil in a large pan and brown the meat in batches. Don't overcrowd the pan, and only turn the meat when it has a deep brown crust on the underside, as this will add lots of flavour to the stew. When one batch is cooked, tip it into the slow cooker and continue with the next batch, adding more oil as you need it.

2 When all the meat has been transferred to the slow cooker, add the onion, carrots and celery to the pan and cook for 5–10 mins to just soften, scraping any meaty bits up from the bottom of the pan. Tip the veg into the slow cooker. Add the lardons to the pan and fry until crispy. Pour in the cider, bubble for 1 min, again scraping the bottom of the pan, then tip the cider and lardons into the slow cooker too. Add the apples, stock cube and herbs to the slow cooker, pour in 400ml/14fl oz water, season well and turn the heat to Low. Cover with the lid and cook for 6–8 hours until the meat is very tender.

3 Turn your slow cooker up to High. Add the crème fraîche and mustard to the stew and check the seasoning. If the sauce is thin, you can thicken it with the cornflour – ladle 2 spoonfuls of the sauce into a pan and bring to a simmer. Mix the cornflour with 1-2 tsp cold water to make a paste, then stir it into the sauce. Once thickened, return the sauce to the slow cooker and cook for 10 mins more on High, stirring occasionally (or for 5 mins on the hob). Serve with mashed potato, greens and extra mustard and thyme, if you like.

PER SERVING 594 kcals, fat 37g, saturates 16g, carbs 19g, sugars 15g, fibre 4g, protein 41g, salt 2.8g

Ginger-beer & Tangerine-glazed Ham

This warming ham is great for entertaining as it's simple to prepare in advance. Many gammons don't need soaking before cooking, but check with your butcher.

1 day, plus 1 hour to finish 8

- 3kg/6lb 8oz mild-cure gammon
- 1 onion, halved
- 3 tangerines, zest removed with a vegetable peeler
- 4 star anise
- 2 litres/3½ pints ginger beer
- small handful cloves

FOR THE GLAZE
- 3 tbsp honey
- 2 tbsp wholegrain mustard

1 Heat the slow cooker if necessary. Put the gammon, onion, tangerine zest and star anise in the pot. Pour over all but 100ml/3½fl oz of the ginger beer and, if necessary, top up with water so the gammon is just covered. Cover and cook for 10 hours on Low until cooked through. Cool, cover and chill at this stage if you want to prepare ahead – bring back to room temperature before continuing.

2 Heat oven to 220C/200C fan/gas 7. Carefully cut the skin off the gammon, making sure to leave a layer of fat, then lightly score the fat into diamond shapes. Put in a roasting tin lined with foil.

3 Warm the honey, mustard and reserved ginger beer in a pan and boil until it thickens. Spoon over the fat, then stud a clove into the middle of each diamond. Bake for 20–25 mins or until the glaze has caramelised. If you did prepare ahead, add another 10 mins to the cooking time. Slice and eat warm or cold.

PER SERVING 451 kcals, fat 27g, saturates 10g, carbs 4g, sugars 4g, fibre none, protein 50g, salt 6.49g

Italian Sausage Stew with Rosemary-garlic Mash

Don't season with salt until cooked and ready to serve. If you salt lentils while cooking, it can prevent them from softening.

 7–9 hours 4

- 8 good-quality pork sausages
- 2 tbsp olive oil
- 2 carrots, finely chopped
- 2 celery sticks, finely chopped
- 1 onion, finely chopped
- 2 rosemary sprigs, 1 chopped
- 3 garlic cloves, roughly chopped
- 175g/6oz dried green lentils, rinsed
- 400g can chopped tomatoes
- 400ml/14fl oz chicken or vegetable stock
- 1kg/2lb 4oz potatoes, cut into chunks
- 150ml/5fl oz milk

1 Heat the slow cooker if necessary. Fry the sausages in 1 tablespoon of the oil in a frying pan until brown. Transfer to the slow cooker pot with the carrots, celery, onion, chopped rosemary, half the garlic and the lentils, tomatoes and stock. Cover and cook on Low for 6–8 hours until the lentils are tender and the sausages are cooked through.

2 Keep warm while you make the mash to serve. Boil the potatoes until tender. Drain them well.

3 Meanwhile, in another pan, heat the milk, remaining garlic and rosemary sprig until just about to boil, then turn off the heat. Sieve the hot milk over the potatoes and mash with the remaining oil, then season. Serve with the stew.

PER SERVING 616 kcals, fat 29g, saturates 8g, carbs 67g, sugars 12g, fibre 9g, protein 27g, salt 3.91g

Venetian Duck Ragu

Like all the best ragus, this one is slowly simmered until the meat is meltingly tender. It's also good value – four duck legs feed six.

 6–7 hours 6

- 1 tbsp olive oil
- 4 duck legs
- 2 onions, finely chopped
- 2 fat garlic cloves, crushed
- 2 tsp ground cinnamon
- 2 tsp plain flour
- 250ml/9fl oz red wine
- 2 x 400g cans chopped tomatoes
- 1 chicken stock cube, made up to 250ml/9fl oz chicken stock
- 3 rosemary sprigs, leaves picked and chopped
- 2 bay leaves
- 1 tsp caster sugar
- 2 tbsp milk
- 600g/1lb 5oz paccheri or pappardelle pasta
- grated Parmesan, to serve

1 Heat the slow cooker if necessary. Heat the oil in a large pan. Add the duck legs and brown on all sides for about 10 mins. Put in the slow cooker pot. Add the onions to the pan and cook for 5 mins until softened. Add the garlic and cook for a further 1 min, then stir in the cinnamon and flour and cook for a further min. Add the wine, tomatoes, stock, herbs, sugar and seasoning. Bring to a simmer, then pour into the pot, cover and cook on Low for 5-6 hours.

2 Carefully lift the duck legs out of the sauce and place on a plate – they will be very tender so try not to lose any of the meat. Pull off and discard the fat, then shred the meat with two forks and discard the bones. If there is a lot of excess oil on the sauce you can skim it off with a spoon. Add the meat back to the sauce with the milk and heat, uncovered, while you cook the pasta.

3 Cook the pasta following pack instructions, then drain, reserving a cup of the pasta water, and add the pasta to the ragu. Stir to coat all the pasta in the sauce, adding a splash of cooking liquid if it looks dry. Serve with grated Parmesan, if you like.

PER SERVING 505 kcals, fat 12g, saturates 2g, carbs 62g, sugars 8g, fibre 2g, protein 30g, salt 0.9g

Duck, Apricot & Pine Nut Pastilla

This pie is worth every bit of effort. It is traditional to dust it with icing sugar.

 3 days 6

- 6 duck legs
- 85g/3oz sea salt
- 600g/1lb 5oz goose or duck fat, melted
- big bottle vegetable oil
- 2 onions, chopped
- 1 tbsp each ground cinnamon and ground cumin, plus pinch extra cinnamon for dusting
- 1 tsp fennel seeds
- tiny pinch saffron
- 140g/5oz dried ready-to-eat apricots, quartered
- 400ml/14fl oz chicken stock
- zest 2 lemons, plus a good squeeze juice
- 50g/2oz toasted pine nuts, plus a few extra to garnish
- 4 large sheets brik or 8 large sheets filo pastry
- 1 tsp icing sugar, for dusting (optional)

1 Rub the duck legs with the salt. Cover and chill overnight.
2 Heat the slow cooker if necessary. Wipe off the salt and put the legs in the pot. If they don't fit, do in batches. Pour over the melted fat, topping up with vegetable oil if the duck isn't covered. Cover and cook on Low for 10–12 hours until tender.
3 Shred the duck meat from the bone, discarding the skin and bones.
4 Fry the onions and spices in a frying pan with a little oil until golden. Stir in the apricots, chicken stock and duck. Cook gently until moist. Add the lemon zest, juice, pine nuts and season.
5 Heat oven to 220C/200C fan/gas 7 with a baking sheet. Brush a 22–23cm round loose-bottomed tin with oil. Line the base and sides with half the pastry sheets. Spoon in the duck mixture. Sit the remaining pastry on top, scrunching the edges. Brush with oil. Bake for 20–30 mins until golden. To serve, scatter with pine nuts and dust with cinnamon and the icing sugar, if using.

PER SERVING 359 kcals, fat 19g, saturates 3g, carbs 26g, sugars 13g, fibre 3g, protein 23g, salt 0.79g

French Duck Confit

In this recipe, duck legs are cooked French-style in goose fat, making them incredibly tender. The dish can be made up to a month ahead and kept in the fridge.

 2 days, plus ½ hour to finish 2

- 25g/1oz sea salt flakes
- 2 tsp crushed black peppercorns
- 4 fresh bay leaves
- 2 large or 4 small duck legs (about 550g/1lb 4oz total)
- 1 tsp thyme leaves, plus 2–4 sprigs
- 340g can goose or duck fat, melted
- 300ml/½ pint groundnut oil

1 At least 24 hours before serving, mix together the salt, pepper and bay leaves. Add the duck legs and rub in the salt. Cover and leave in the fridge.

2 Next day, heat the slow cooker if necessary. Wipe the salt from the duck and put the legs in a single layer in the slow cooker pot. Add the thyme, plus the bay and peppercorns from the salt and pour over the melted fat. If it doesn't cover the duck, top up with groundnut oil. Cover and cook on Low for 10–12 hours. The duck skin should be creamy.

3 Transfer the legs to a bowl and strain in the fat, pushing the duck under until fully submerged. (This can now be refrigerated for up to 1 month.)

4 Heat oven to 220C/200C fan/gas 7. Remove the duck legs from the fat, wiping off any excess. Season and sit the legs on a wire rack in a roasting tin. Cook for 30 mins until the skin is crisp (for a really crispy skin, flash under a hot grill for a few mins at the end).

PER SERVING 529 kcals, fat 38g, saturates 12g, carbs 1g, sugars none, fibre none, protein 43g, salt 1.37g

Pot-roast Pheasant with Cider & Bacon

Cider and cream elevate this homely pot-roast to a dish ready to grace a dinner party.

 7–9 hours 4

- 50g/2oz butter
- 2 pheasants, cleaned
- 100g/4oz bacon lardons
- 1 onion, chopped
- 1 celery stick, chopped
- 4 sage sprigs, leaves chopped
- 2 eating apples, cored and cut into large chunks
- 500ml/18fl oz cider
- 300ml/½ pint chicken stock
- 1 Savoy cabbage, finely shredded
- 100ml/3½fl oz double cream
- mashed potato, to serve (optional)

1 Heat the slow cooker if necessary. Melt the butter in a large frying pan. Season the pheasants, add to the pan and brown on all sides. Transfer to the slow cooker pot. Add the bacon and onion to the frying pan and cook until the onion is soft and the bacon crisp. Tip into the pot with the celery, sage, apples, cider and stock.

2 Cover and cook on Low for 6–8 hours or until the pheasants are cooked through and tender. Turn the pheasants halfway through.

3 Remove the birds from the dish and keep warm. Strain the remaining contents into a big pan. Tip the contents of the sieve into a serving dish. Boil the liquid until reduced by just over half, then add the cabbage, cover with a lid and cook for 3 mins. Add the cream, check the seasoning, and continue cooking for 1 min more. Pour over the reserved bacon-and-apple mixture, and stir together. Sit the pheasants on top and serve with mashed potato, if you like.

PER SERVING 865 kcals, fat 56g, saturates 26g, carbs 15g, sugars 15g, fibre 6g, protein 67g, salt 1.6g

Steamed Venison & Port Pudding

Serve whole for extra wow factor, then slice into the pudding in front of your guests.

🕐 7-8 hours, plus chilling 4

- 600g/1lb 5oz cubed stewing venison, such as shoulder
- 140g/5oz cubed belly pork, skin on
- 2 tbsp beef dripping or lard, plus extra for greasing
- 1 onion, finely sliced
- 1 tbsp plain flour
- 1 tsp thyme leaves, chopped
- 2 tbsp mushroom ketchup
- 100ml/3½fl oz port
- 50ml/2fl oz red wine
- 125ml/4fl oz good beef stock

FOR THE PASTRY
- 375g/13oz self-raising flour
- 140g/5oz shredded suet
- 1 tsp salt

1 Mix the pastry ingredients. Add 250ml/9fl oz cold water gradually to the dough. Wrap in cling film and chill.

2 Brown the venison and pork in batches in 1 tablespoon of the dripping. Set aside. Add the remaining dripping to the pan, then the onion. Soften. Return the meat to the pan, stir in the flour, thyme, ketchup, port, wine and stock. Simmer, season and cool.

3 To assemble, grease a 1-litre pudding basin. Roll out two-thirds of the pastry to a circle to line the basin. Add the filling, pressing it down. Roll out the remaining pastry to make a lid. Moisten the edges with water, stick on the lid and pinch to seal. Cover with a double layer of greased foil and baking parchment, folding a pleat in the sheets. Tie on with string.

4 Sit a trivet in the base of the slow cooker – try a small upturned saucer. Sit the pudding on top and pour boiling water to halfway up the basin. Cover and cook on High for 5–6 hours, until a skewer poked into the pudding comes out piping hot.

5 Turn out and serve.

PER SERVING 1,091 kcals, fat 60g, saturates 29g, carbs 81g, sugars 8g, fibre 5g, protein 47g, salt 2.7g

Venison Sausage & Chestnut Casserole

You can't go wrong with this warming casserole, with its rich red wine sauce and chestnuts.

 4 hours   8

- 2 tbsp sunflower oil
- 16 venison sausages
- 2 medium onions, thinly sliced
- 3 celery sticks, trimmed and thinly sliced
- 200g/7oz chestnut mushrooms, halved (or quartered if large)
- 300ml/½ pint red wine
- 1 beef stock cube
- 2 tbsp plain flour
- 200g pack vacuum-packed cooked chestnuts
- 2 tbsp tomato purée
- 1 bay leaf
- handful parsley, chopped, to serve
- mustard mash, to serve

1 Heat the slow cooker if necessary. Heat 1 tablespoon of the oil in a large non-stick frying pan and fry the sausages in two batches over a medium heat for 15 mins, turning regularly, until nicely browned. Transfer the sausages to the slow cooker pot.

2 Tip the onions and celery into the frying pan and cook over a medium-high heat for 5 mins or until beginning to soften and lightly colour, stirring regularly. Add a splash more oil if needed. Tip the vegetables into the pot with the raw mushrooms.

3 Pour the wine and 300ml/½ pint water into the pan and crumble the stock cube over the top. Bring to the boil, then tip in the flour mixed with 3 tablespoons cold water and stir until smooth. Stir in the chestnuts, tomato purée and bay leaf. Tip into the pot, stir, then cover and cook on Low for 4 hours. Season and sprinkle with chopped parsley, if using. Serve with mash.

PER SERVING 591 kcals, fat 27g, saturates 14g, carbs 52g, sugars 7g, fibre 7g, protein 25g, salt 1.8g

Rich Paprika Seafood Bowl

This easy seafood stew makes a nice lunch or light supper with a big chunk of crusty bread to mop up the sauce.

 9–11½ hours 4

- large bunch flat-leaf parsley, leaves and stalks separated
- 1 tbsp olive oil
- 2 onions, halved and thinly sliced
- 2 celery sticks, finely chopped
- 2–3 tsp paprika
- 200g/7oz roasted red peppers, thickly sliced
- 400g can chopped tomatoes with garlic
- few fresh mussels (optional)
- 400g/14oz white fish fillet, cut into very large chunks
- crusty bread, to serve

1 Heat the slow cooker if necessary. Put the parsley stalks, half the leaves, oil and some seasoning into a food processor, and whizz to a paste. Add this and the onions, celery, paprika, peppers and chopped tomatoes to the slow cooker pot. Give everything a good stir, then cover and cook on Low for 8–10 hours.

2 If using the mussels, nestle these into the sauce and scatter the fish on top. Re-cover, then cook on High for 30 mins–1 hour until the fish is just flaking and the mussels have opened – discard any that stay shut. Gently stir the seafood into the sauce, season, then serve in bowls with a scattering of the remaining parsley.

PER SERVING 192 kcals, fat 7g, saturates 1g, carbs 12g, sugars 8g, fibre 4g, protein 22g, salt 1.14g

Tender Summer Squid with Aioli

The long slow cooking in this recipe is worth it for really tender squid. It is topped with a cheat's aioli using bought mayonnaise.

 4 hours 4

FOR THE STEW
- 215g pack cooking chorizo, skin removed
- 1 onion, finely chopped
- few thyme sprigs, leaves only
- 1 tsp sweet smoked paprika, plus a little for the aïoli
- 50ml/2fl oz dry white wine
- 450g/1lb cherry vine tomatoes
- 450g/1lb large new potatoes, peeled and cut into bite-sized chunks
- 500g/1lb 2oz prepared squid, tubes cut into rings, plus tentacles
- small pack flat-leaf parsley, leaves roughly chopped

FOR THE AIOLI
- 1 garlic clove, crushed
- 4 tbsp good mayonnaise, ideally olive oil-based
- squeeze of lemon juice, plus extra to serve
- crusty bread, to serve

1 Heat the slow cooker if necessary. Heat a large pan. Add the chorizo and fry for 5 mins, using a wooden spoon to break it up, until golden and oozing with oil. Add the onion and thyme and soften for 5 mins.

2 Stir in the paprika, cook for 1 min, then splash in the wine, 50ml/2fl oz water and the tomatoes and potatoes. Tip into the slow cooker pot and stir in the squid, then cover and cook on Low for 3½ hours until the squid is very tender.

3 Meanwhile, mix the garlic, mayo and lemon juice, then set aside. Sprinkle with a little paprika, if you like.

4 Stir the parsley into the stew and serve portions with a dollop of the aïoli, a squeeze of lemon and some crusty bread.

PER SERVING 545 kcals, fat 33g, saturates 9g, carbs 29g, sugars 8g, fibre 4g, protein 33g, salt 1.4g

Sea Bass & Seafood Italian One-pot

Just plonk this dish in the middle of the table, lift off the lid and your guests will realise that impressive food doesn't have to be fussy or fancy.

 3-4 hours 4

- 2 tbsp olive oil
- 1 fennel bulb, halved and sliced, fronds kept to garnish
- 2 garlic cloves, sliced
- ½ red chilli, deseeded and chopped
- 250g/9oz prepared squid, sliced into rings
- bunch basil, leaves and stalks separated, stalks tied together, leaves roughly torn
- 400g can chopped tomatoes
- 75ml/2½fl oz white wine
- 2 large handfuls mussels or clams
- 8 large raw prawns
- 4 sea bass fillets (about 140g/5oz each)
- crusty bread, to serve

1 Heat the slow cooker if necessary. Mix the oil, fennel, garlic, chilli, squid, basil stalks, tomatoes and wine in the slow cooker pot. Cover and cook on High for 2–3 hours until the squid and the fennel are tender.

2 Scatter the mussels or clams and the prawns over the sauce, lay the sea bass fillets on top, cover and cook for 30–45 mins more until the mussels or clams have opened and the fish is cooked through and flakes easily. You can keep an eye on the fish through the lid to ensure it doesn't overcook.

3 Serve scattered with the basil leaves and fennel fronds, and eat with crusty bread.

PER SERVING 329 kcals, fat 11g, saturates 2g, carbs 7g, sugars 4g, fibre 2g, protein 45g, salt 1g

Sea Bass with Black Bean Sauce

This dish is perfect for a special meal for two, as it's really impressive but actually dead easy to make.

 1½ hours 2

- 1 sea bass, head on, gutted
- 2cm/¾in piece ginger, peeled and thinly sliced
- 2 tbsp Shaohsing rice wine
- 100ml/3½fl oz black bean sauce
- 2 spring onions, shredded
- small handful coriander, leaves only
- jasmine rice, to serve

1 Wash the fish in cold running water, pat dry with kitchen paper, then slash three or four slits into the skin on both sides. Season all over with salt and ground white pepper. Put ginger slices in the slits of the fish and inside the cavity. Put the fish on an upturned plate that fits inside your slow cooker. Turn the cooker to High and add the rice wine. Cover and cook on High for an hour without taking off the lid.

2 While the fish is cooking, heat the black bean sauce following the pack instructions and stir in 2 tablespoons water to thin it a little.

3 Carefully remove the fish. Drizzle with the sauce, and scatter with the spring onions and coriander leaves. Serve with jasmine rice.

PER SERVING 511 kcals, fat 29g, saturates 5g, carbs 11g, sugars 8g, fibre 1g, protein 49g, salt 7.67g

Fish Mappas

This coconut fish curry, popular in the southern Indian state of Kerala, works for a casual supper with friends, but the family will love it too.

 6 hours 4

- 1 tbsp sunflower oil
- 2 large onions, sliced
- 2 garlic cloves, chopped
- 450g/1lb tomatoes, cut into chunks
- 3 tbsp tikka curry paste
- 1 vegetable stock cube, crumbled
- 400g can coconut milk
- 4 skinless pollock fillets (about 150g/5½oz each), or other sustainable white fish, cut into 4cm/1½in chunks
- ½ small pack coriander, roughly chopped
- 300g/11oz basmati rice, boiled

1 Heat the slow cooker if necessary. Heat the oil in a large, wide saucepan over a medium heat and add the onions and garlic and cook for 5 mins. Tip into the slow cooker pot and add the tomatoes, curry paste, stock cube and coconut milk. Cover and cook on Low for 5 hours until the onions are soft.
2 Add the fish to the pot and cook for 30 mins more until the fish flakes. Sprinkle the coriander over the curry and serve with the rice.

PER SERVING 691 kcals, fat 26g, saturates 16g, carbs 74g, sugars 11g, fibre 4g, protein 39g, salt 0.8g

Chapter 5:

VEGETARIAN & VEGETABLES

Italian Vegetable Bake

Layer this up straight into your slow cooker pot then flash under the grill after cooking to brown the top.

 6-7 hours 6

- 4 garlic cloves, 3 crushed, 1 left whole
- 400g can chopped tomatoes
- bunch oregano, leaves chopped
- large pinch dried chilli flakes
- about 300g/11oz baby or normal aubergines, sliced
- 2 courgettes, sliced
- ½ large jar roasted red peppers
- 3 beef tomatoes, sliced
- bunch basil, torn (save a few leaves for sprinkling over)
- small baguette, sliced and toasted
- 2 x 125g balls mozzarella, torn
- green salad, to serve

1 Heat the slow cooker on High. Tip in the crushed garlic, canned tomatoes, half the oregano leaves, chilli and some seasoning. Cook, covered, while you chop the rest of the vegetables.

2 Tip out most of the tomato sauce mix from the pot and start layering up half the vegetables and herbs with seasoning – the aubergines, courgettes, red peppers, tomatoes, basil and remaining oregano. Layer in half the bread, rubbed with the whole garlic clove, half the mozzarella and half the tipped-out tomato sauce. Repeat vegetable, herb and tomato sauce layers, followed by the bread and mozzarella. Push everything down well to compress, then cook on high for 5-6 hours.

3 Flash under the grill before serving if you like (and your slow cooker pot is suitable), until golden and bubbling. Serve with the leftover basil leaves on top and a big salad on the side.

PER SERVING 274 kcals, fat 10g, saturates 6g, carbs 31g, sugars 8g, fibre 4g, protein 14g, salt 0.9g

Macaroni Cheese

This is a really clever recipe that needs no fiddly white sauce and still results in a creamy version of this family classic.

 1 hour 4

- 25g/1oz cornflour
- 700ml/1¼ pints semi-skimmed milk
- 200ml/7fl oz crème fraîche
- 1 heaped tsp English mustard powder
- 1 large garlic clove, finely chopped
- 1 bay leaf
- generous pinch crushed dried chillies
- freshly grated nutmeg
- 250g/9oz macaroni
- 140g/5oz extra mature cheddar, grated
- 50g/2oz fresh breadcrumbs
- 50g/2oz Parmesan, grated
- 450g/1lb mix of tomatoes, such as cherry and medium vine, halved
- bunch spring onions, ends trimmed, sliced

1 Mix the cornflour to a paste with a splash of the milk in a big pan, then gradually stir in the rest of the milk, followed by the crème fraîche, mustard powder, garlic, bay, chillies and nutmeg. Bring to the boil, then turn off and leave to infuse for 5 mins. Heat the slow cooker if necessary.
2 Strain the sauce into the slow cooker pot and stir in the macaroni and cheddar. Cover and cook on High for 30 mins or until the pasta is cooked.
3 Heat grill to high. Pour the pasta into an ovenproof dish and scatter over the breadcrumbs, Parmesan, tomatoes and spring onions. Grill until crisp and golden.

PER SERVING 789 kcals, fat 42g, saturates 25g, carbs 77g, sugars 16g, fibre 4g, protein 31g, salt 1.4g

Golden Veggie Shepherd's Pie

Dried lentils are cheap and nutritious; we've used green here, but red work just as well. Never add salt to lentils while they are cooking, though – it toughens their skins.

 6-7 hours   10  easily halved

- 50g/2oz butter
- 2 onions, chopped
- 4 carrots, diced
- 1 celery head, chopped
- 4 garlic cloves, finely chopped
- 200g pack chestnut mushrooms, sliced
- 2 bay leaves
- 1 tbsp dried thyme
- 500g pack dried green lentils
- 100ml/4fl oz red wine (optional)
- 1.7 litres/3 pints vegetable stock
- 3 tbsp tomato purée
- 2kg/4lb 8oz mashed potato
- 50g/2oz cheddar, grated

1 Heat the slow cooker if necessary. Heat the butter in a pan, then gently fry the onions, carrots, celery and garlic for 15 mins until soft and golden. Tip into the slow cooker pot and stir in the mushrooms, herbs and lentils. Pour over the wine, if using, and stock, cover and cook on High for 5–6 hours – do not season with salt at this stage.

2 Now season to taste, turn off the slow cooker and stir in the tomato purée. Divide the lentil mixture among one, two or individual ovenproof dishes, then top with the mash and scatter over the cheese. If the mash is cold, bake the dish in a hot oven for 30 mins until piping hot, or if using hot mash, just grill until golden and starting to crisp.

PER SERVING 449 kcals, fat 13g, saturates 7g, carbs 68g, sugars 9g, fibre 10g, protein 19g, salt 0.59g

Veggie Moussaka

The lentils, sweet potatoes and aubergine are all cooked together in the slow cooker in this low-fat moussaka, then it is finished in the oven.

🕐 5 hours   ◔ 4-6

- 1 tbsp sunflower oil
- 2 onions, halved and sliced
- 2 garlic cloves, chopped
- 2 bay leaves
- 1 tsp dried oregano
- ½ tsp each cinnamon and allspice
- 400g can chopped tomatoes
- 1 tbsp tomato purée
- 140g/5oz dried green lentils
- 1 vegetable stock cube
- 200g/7oz sweet potatoes, thickly sliced
- 1 large aubergine, sliced and the biggest slices halved again
- 250g/9oz low-fat fromage frais
- 1 large egg
- 50g/2oz feta, crumbled
- 4 tomatoes, thickly sliced

1 Heat the slow cooker if necessary. Heat the oil in a large pan and fry the onions and garlic for about 10 mins until golden. Stir in the herbs and spices, then tip in the tomatoes and tomato purée, lentils and stock cube with 500ml/18fl oz water. Add the sweet potato and aubergine, then tip into the slow cooker and cook on Low for 4 hours until the lentils are tender and pulpy. Take off the lid when it is ready to release any excess steam. Remove the bay leaves.

2 Heat oven to 180C/160C fan/gas 4. Beat the fromage frais, egg and cheese together. Tip the lentil mixture into a large ovenproof dish, cover with the cheese mixture, then arrange the tomatoes on top. Grind over some black pepper and bake for 25 mins until the topping is set.

PER SERVING (6) 213 kcals, fat 4g, saturates 2g, carbs 30g, sugars 13g, fibre 9g, protein 15g, salt 1.0g

Black Bean Chilli

This vegetarian chilli can bubble happily away while you're out for the day, then when you get home you can enjoy a low-fat supper containing all your five-a-day.

 8½ hours   4-6 easily halved or doubled

- 2 tbsp olive oil
- 4 garlic cloves, finely chopped
- 2 large onions, chopped
- 3 tbsp smoked sweet paprika or mild chilli powder
- 3 tbsp ground cumin
- 3 tbsp cider vinegar
- 2 tbsp brown sugar
- 2 x 400g cans chopped tomatoes
- 2 x 400g cans black beans, drained and rinsed
- rice, to serve, plus a few, or one, of the following – crumbled feta, chopped spring onions, sliced radishes, avocado chunks, soured cream

1 Heat the slow cooker if necessary. Heat the olive oil in a frying pan and fry the garlic and onions for 5 mins until almost softened.

2 Add the paprika or chilli and cumin, cook for a few mins, then scrape into the slow cooker pot with the vinegar, sugar, tomatoes, beans and some seasoning. Cover and cook on Low for 8 hours. Serve with rice and the accompaniments of your choice in small bowls.

PER SERVING 339 kcals, fat 10g, saturates 1g, carbs 50g, sugars 20g, fibre 8g, protein 17g, salt 1.45g

Greek Butter Bean & Tomato Stew

This veggie main meal also doubles as a great side dish to serve with roast lamb.

 3½-4½ hours    6   easily halved

- 4 x 400g cans butter beans
- 100ml/3½fl oz Greek extra virgin olive oil
- 3 small red onions, finely sliced
- 2 large carrots, finely sliced
- 3 celery stalks with leaves, finely chopped
- 4 -6 sundried tomatoes, sliced
- 1kg/2lb 4oz ripe tomatoes, skinned, deseeded and finely chopped
- 4 garlic cloves, chopped
- 1 tsp paprika
- ½-1 tsp ground cinnamon
- 2 tbsp tomato purée
- 1 tsp sugar
- small pack flat-leaf parsley, finely chopped
- small pack dill, finely chopped
- 100g/4oz feta (optional), crumbled

1 Heat the slow cooker if necessary. Drain the canned beans, reserving the liquid. Heat the oil in a large pan and cook the onions, carrots and celery for a few mins. Stir in the remaining ingredients with 300ml/½ pint bean juice, reserving half of the chopped herbs and feta, if using.
2 Bring to the boil, tip into the slow cooker, cover and cook on Low for 3-4 hours, stirring once.
3 Stir through the reserved chopped herbs, season to taste, then crumble over the remaining feta just before serving.

PER SERVING 315 kcals, fat 18g, saturates 3g, carbs 24g, sugars 2g, fibre 11g, protein 8g, salt 1.1g

Mumbai Potato Wraps with Minted Yogurt Relish

These spicy potatoes are fantastic in Indian-style wraps, but you can just as easily spoon them over rice, or serve in bowls with a wedge of naan bread to dunk in.

 3½ hours 4 easily halved

- 1 onion, sliced
- 2 tbsp medium curry powder
- 400g can chopped tomatoes
- 750g/1lb 10oz potatoes, diced
- 2 tbsp mango chutney, plus extra to taste (optional)
- 100g/4oz low-fat natural yogurt
- 1 tsp mint sauce from a jar
- 8 plain chapattis
- small bunch coriander, to garnish

1 Heat the slow cooker if necessary. Tip the onion, curry powder, chopped tomatoes, potatoes and mango chutney into the slow cooker pot with 50ml/2fl oz boiling water. Stir everything together, then cover and cook for 3 hours on High until the potatoes are tender. Season.

2 Meanwhile, mix together the yogurt and mint sauce, and warm the chapattis following the pack instructions.

3 To serve, spoon some of the potatoes on to a chapatti and top with a few sprigs of coriander. Drizzle with the minted yogurt relish, adding extra mango chutney, if you wish, then roll up and eat.

PER SERVING 426 kcals, fat 7g, saturates 1g, carbs 83g, sugars 12g, fibre 6g, protein 14g, salt 1.22g

Summary Vegetables & Chickpeas

Tomato-based stews like this are perfect for slow cookers and ideal for making ahead. Vary the vegetables depending on what's in your fridge or in season.

 6½–8½ hours   4   easily halved

- 3 courgettes, thickly sliced
- 1 aubergine, cut into chunks
- 3 garlic cloves, chopped
- 2 red peppers, deseeded and chopped into chunks
- 2 large baking potatoes, peeled and cut into bite-sized chunks
- 1 onion, chopped
- 1 tbsp coriander seeds
- 4 tbsp olive oil
- 400g can chopped tomatoes
- 400g can chickpeas, drained and rinsed
- small bunch coriander, roughly chopped
- crusty bread, to serve

1 Heat the slow cooker if necessary. Tip all of the vegetables into the slow cooker pot and toss with the coriander seeds, most of the olive oil and some salt and pepper. Pour over the tomatoes and chickpeas, then cover and cook on Low for 6–8 hours until the potatoes are tender.
2 Season to taste, drizzle with the remaining olive oil, then scatter over the coriander. Serve from the pot or pile into a serving dish. Eat with hunks of crusty bread.

PER SERVING 327 kcals, fat 15g, saturates 2g, carbs 40g, sugars 13g, fibre 9g, protein 11g, salt 0.51g

Smoky Aubergine Tagine with Lemon & Apricots

Aubergines have a natural 'meaty' quality that will please even those who think they don't like meat-free dishes. Add a can of chickpeas if you want it to be more substantial.

 2½ hours 4

- 2 aubergines, cut into large chunks
- 3 tbsp olive oil
- 2 onions, chopped
- 2 tbsp freshly grated ginger
- 1½ tsp each ras el hanout and smoked sweet paprika
- good pinch of saffron
- 300ml/½ pint hot vegetable stock
- 1 preserved lemon, chopped (optional)
- 120g/4½oz ready-to-eat dried apricots, halved
- 200g/7oz tomatoes, roughly chopped
- 1 tbsp clear honey
- zest and juice 1 lemon
- 2 tsp toasted sesame seeds
- 2 tbsp each finely chopped flat-leaf parsley and mint
- Greek yogurt and wholegrain bulghar wheat, to serve (optional)

1 Heat the slow cooker if necessary. Brown the aubergines in 2 tablespoons of the oil so they're golden on all sides, but not soft in the middle yet – this is best done in batches in a large, non-stick frying pan.

2 Heat a heavy-based shallow lidded pan or flameproof tagine with the remaining oil, then add the onions, ginger and spices and fry gently until softened and golden. Tip into the slow cooker.

3 Meanwhile, add the saffron to the stock to soak. Stir the preserved lemon, if using, apricots, tomatoes, honey and lemon juice into the onions with the saffron stock. Pour over the aubergines, cover and cook on High for 2 hours until the aubergines are tender. Season to taste.

4 Mix together the lemon zest, sesame seeds and chopped herbs, and sprinkle over the tagine. Serve with Greek yogurt and wholegrain bulghar wheat, if you like.

PER SERVING 270 kcals, fat 11g, saturates 2g, carbs 29g, sugars 26g, fibre 12g, protein 8g, salt 0.3g

Cauliflower Cheese & Spinach Pasta Bakes

Somewhere between macaroni cheese and cauliflower cheese, these pasta bakes are perfect for a cold day when only a really satisfying supper will do.

 2½–3 hours   6   easily halved

- 50g/2oz melted butter, plus 1 tbsp
- 50g/2oz plain flour
- 700ml/1¼ pints milk
- 1 tsp Dijon mustard
- 100g/4oz extra mature cheddar, grated
- 25–50g/1–2oz blue cheese
- ½ tsp finely grated nutmeg
- 1kg/2lb 4oz cauliflower (2 medium ones), cut into florets
- 250g/9oz penne
- 4 handfuls spinach leaves
- 300g/10oz tomato pasta sauce
- 25g/1oz toasted pine nuts
- green salad or garlic bread, to serve

1 Heat the slow cooker if necessary. Stir together the butter and flour in the slow cooker pot, then gradually whisk in the milk and mustard. Stir in most of the cheddar, half of the blue cheese, the nutmeg and the cauliflower with some seasoning. Cover and cook on High for 1 hour until the cauliflower is almost tender. Add the pasta, mixing well so that it is covered by the sauce (add a splash more milk if you need to), and cook for a further 30 mins–1 hour until the pasta is cooked.

2 Heat grill to high. Stir through the spinach to wilt, then spoon half into an ovenproof dish or six individual dishes. Dollop the tomato sauce over the top, then spoon the rest of the cauliflower– pasta mixture over the tomato sauce. Scatter with the remaining cheeses and the pine nuts, and grill until golden and bubbling. Good with a green salad or garlic bread.

PER SERVING 515 kcals, fat 25g, saturates 12g, carbs 54g, sugars 15 g, fibre 6g, protein 23g, salt 1.28g

Sweet Potato & Spinach Bake

If you want to make this dish healthier, swap the double cream for single, or use half-fat crème fraîche. It will look a little split and grainy, but it will still taste great.

 2½ hours   4

- 300ml/½ pint double cream
- 1 garlic clove, peeled
- 2 thyme or rosemary sprigs
- 250g bag frozen spinach
- freshly grated nutmeg
- butter, for greasing
- 850g/1lb 14oz sweet potatoes, peeled and thinly sliced (about 3mm thick)
- 25g/1oz grated hard cheese, such as cheddar, Parmesan or a veggie alternative

1 Remove the slow cooker pot and heat the base if necessary. Put the cream, garlic and herb sprigs into a small pan and slowly bring to just below boiling. Turn off the heat, season and leave to infuse.

2 Put the spinach into a colander, pour over a kettle of boiling water and leave to drain for a few mins. Then squeeze out as much water as possible. Season with some salt, pepper and the freshly grated nutmeg.

3 Grease the pot of the slow cooker generously with butter and spread half the sweet potato slices across the bottom. Top with a layer of spinach, then the remaining potato. Pour over the cream mixture through a sieve, to remove the garlic and herbs, then sprinkle with the cheese. Cover and bake for 2 hours on High until tender. If you like, remove the pot and grill to crisp up the top.

PER SERVING 611 kcals, fat 45g, saturates 25g, carbs 48g, sugars 14g, fibre 7g, protein 7g, salt 0.61g

Lentil Ragout

This sauce is also great spooned over jacket potatoes, or into halved peppers then topped with grated cheddar and baked in the oven.

 7½–9½ hours 6

- 3 tbsp olive oil
- 2 onions, finely chopped
- 3 carrots, finely chopped
- 3 celery sticks, finely chopped
- 3 garlic cloves, crushed
- 2 x 400g cans chopped tomatoes
- 2 tbsp tomato purée
- 2 tsp each dried oregano and thyme
- 3 bay leaves
- 500g bag dried red lentils
- 500ml/18fl oz vegetable stock
- 500g/1lb 2oz spaghetti
- grated Parmesan, to serve

1 Heat the slow cooker if necessary. Mix the oil, onions, carrots, celery, garlic, chopped tomatoes, purée and herbs in the slow cooker pot. Cover and cook on Low for 6–7 hours.

2 Stir in the lentils and stock, and cook on High for 1–2 hours until the lentils are tender. Season.

3 If eating straight away, keep on a low heat while you cook the spaghetti, according to the pack instructions. Drain well, divide among pasta bowls or plates, spoon the sauce over the top and grate over some cheese. Alternatively, cool the sauce and chill for up to 3 days or freeze it in portions for up to 3 months. Simply defrost overnight at room temperature, then reheat gently to serve.

PER SERVING 662 kcals, fat 9g, saturates 1g, carbs 120g, sugars 14g, fibre 10g, protein 33g, salt 1.05g

Creamy Black Dhal with Toppings

This freezes well, so you could make a big batch. Add toppings for a bit of colour and texture like crispy fried onions, chutneys, yogurt and herbs and pickles.

 5½-6½ hours, plus soaking  4 ◑ easily doubled

- 250g/9oz black urid beans (also called urid dal, urad dal, black lentils or black gram beans) – yellow split peas also work well
- 100g/4oz butter or ghee
- 2 large onions, halved and thinly sliced
- 3 garlic cloves, crushed
- thumb-sized piece ginger, peeled and finely chopped
- 2 tsp each ground cumin and coriander
- 1 tsp each turmeric and paprika
- ¼ tsp chilli powder (optional)
- small bunch coriander, stalks finely chopped, leaves reserved to serve
- 400g/14oz passata or chopped tomatoes
- 1 fat red chilli, pierced a few times with the tip of a sharp knife
- 50ml/2fl oz double cream

TO SERVE
- rice, naan bread or baked sweet potatoes
- coriander, sliced red chilli, lime wedges, yogurt (or a swirl of cream), your favourite Indian pickles or chutney, crispy onions

1 Soak the beans in cold water for 4 hours (or overnight, if you like).
2 Heat the slow cooker if necessary. Melt the butter or ghee in a large pan, then add the onions, garlic and ginger and cook slowly for 10–15 mins until the onions are starting to caramelise. Stir in the spices, coriander stalks and 100ml/4fl oz water, bring to the boil and pour into the slow cooker. Add the passata and whole red chilli. Drain the beans and add these too, then top up with 400ml/14fl oz water. Season well, set the slow cooker to Low and cook for 5–6 hours .
3 Once cooked, the dhal should be very thick and the beans tender. Stir in the cream, check the seasoning and serve in bowls with naan bread, rice or in a jacket potato, with your choice of toppings.

PER SERVING 527 kcals, fat 34g, saturates 21g, carbs 35g, sugars 9g, fibre 6g, protein 19g, salt 0.1g

Vegetable Couscous with Chickpeas & Preserved Lemons

Moroccan cooking makes a great use of humble vegetables like potatoes, carrots and parsnips. The broth on it's own seems a bit thin, but is transformed by the couscous.

 4½-5 hours   8   easily halved

FOR THE BROTH
- 1½ litres/2¾ pints vegetable stock
- 3 tbsp harissa
- 3 carrots, chopped
- 3 large parsnips, chopped
- 2 red onions, cut into wedges through the root
- 2 large potatoes, chopped into chunks
- ½ butternut squash, chopped into chunks
- 4 leeks, sliced into rings
- 8-12 dried figs, halved
- 2 preserved lemons, rinsed, pulp scooped out and peel finely sliced
- small bunch mint, chopped

FOR THE COUSCOUS
- 200g/7oz couscous
- 400g can chickpeas
- 25g/1oz butter
- 1 red onion, finely diced
- 3 spring onions, sliced
- 2 tbsp harissa
- 50ml/2fl oz olive oil
- juice 1 lemon
- bunch coriander, roughly chopped

1 Heat the slow cooker if necessary (it needs to be a big one). For the broth, bring the stock to a simmer in a large pan. Add the harissa, vegetables and figs, bring back to the boil and tip into the slow cooker. Cover and cook on High for 4–4½ hours until the vegetables are tender.

2 For the couscous, put the couscous and half the chickpeas into a bowl, add the butter and season. Pour 350ml/12fl oz boiling water over the couscous, cover with cling film, leave aside for 10 mins, then fluff up with a fork.

3 In a separate bowl, combine the red onion, spring onions, harissa, olive oil, remaining chickpeas, lemon juice and coriander, then mix into the couscous. Pile onto a large deep serving dish, ladle over the braised vegetables and broth, and sprinkle with the preserved lemons and chopped mint.

PER SERVING 418 kcals, fat 13g, saturates 3g, carbs 62g, sugars 28g, fibre 11g, protein 9g, salt 1.6g

Veg & Cheesy Rice Bake

This is a great midweek supper that kids will love. It's a satisfying summer dish – particularly if you're a keen gardener and have a glut of crops to use up!

 7½–8½ hours 4

- 1 onion, chopped
- 1 tbsp olive oil
- 2 courgettes, sliced
- 1 aubergine, diced
- 450g/1lb fresh tomatoes, chopped (or 400g can chopped tomatoes)
- 200g/7oz risotto rice
- 2 eggs
- 140g/5oz cheddar, grated

1 Heat the slow cooker if necessary. Mix the onion, oil, courgettes, aubergine and tomatoes in the pot. Cover and cook on Low for 6–8 hours until the aubergine is tender.

2 Heat oven to 200C/180C fan/gas 6. Cook the rice in a large pot of salted boiling water for 20 mins, or until tender. Drain and mix with the eggs and two-thirds of the cheese.

3 Transfer the vegetable mix to an ovenproof dish. Spoon over the rice mixture and smooth out. Sprinkle over the rest of the cheese and bake for 30 mins until bubbling and golden.

PER SERVING 443 kcals, fat 19g, saturates 9g, carbs 48g, sugars 8g, fibre 6g, protein 20g, salt 0.8g

Mushroom, Shallot & Squash Pie

This pie makes a great Sunday lunch for vegetarians. If you don't need to serve six people, assemble individual pies, cook as many as you need and freeze the rest.

 6½–7½ hours 6

- 25g/1oz dried porcini mushrooms
- 600g/1lb 5oz shallots, halved
- 250g/9oz fresh mushrooms, sliced
- 1 tbsp olive oil
- 50g/2oz butter
- 50g/2oz plain flour, plus a little extra for dusting
- 2 garlic cloves, finely chopped
- 2 tsp finely chopped rosemary leaves
- 2 tsp finely chopped sage leaves
- 1 large butternut squash, peeled, deseeded and cut into chunks
- 250ml/9fl oz vegetable stock
- 500g pack puff pastry
- 1 egg, beaten

1 Heat the slow cooker if necessary. Soak the dried mushrooms in 250ml/9fl oz boiling water. Meanwhile, fry the shallots and sliced mushrooms in the olive oil and butter until the shallots have softened. Stir in the flour. Scrape into the slow cooker pot and stir in the garlic and herbs.
2 Strain the dried mushrooms over the slow cooker, stirring their soaking liquid into the shallot mixture well. Roughly chop the porcini and add to the pot too with the squash and stock. Cover and cook on Low for 5–7 hours until the squash is tender.
3 Transfer the mixture to a pie dish.
4 Roll out the pastry on a floured surface until big enough to cover the pie dish. Cover the pie, trimming the excess pastry. Heat oven to 200C/180C fan/ gas 6, glaze the pastry with a little egg and bake for 30–40 mins or until golden and hot through.

PER SERVING 610 kcals, fat 42g, saturates 21g, carbs 51g, sugars 12g, fibre 7g, protein 12g, salt 1.32g

Spicy Spaghetti with Garlic Mushrooms

A spicy pasta supper, perfect for vegetarians, or just for a tasty, healthy dinner.

 8 hours 4  easily doubled

- 2 tbsp olive oil
- 1 garlic clove, thinly sliced
- 1 onion, finely chopped
- 1 celery stick, finely chopped
- 400g can chopped tomatoes
- ½ red chilli, deseeded and finely chopped (or use dried chilli flakes)
- 250g pack chestnut mushrooms, thickly sliced
- 300g/10oz spaghetti
- small bunch parsley, leaves only, to garnish

1 Heat the slow cooker if necessary. Mix all the ingredients except for the pasta and parsley in the slow cooker. Cover and cook on Low for 6–7 hours.
2 Just before you're ready to eat, cook the spaghetti according to the pack instructions. Drain well, tip back in to the cooking pan and stir in the mushroom sauce. Scatter with parsley and serve.

PER SERVING 346 kcals, fat 7g, saturates 1g, carbs 62g, sugars 7g, fibre 5g, protein 12g, salt 0.35g

Pasta with Creamy Greens & Lemon

You can use whatever soft herbs you like in this dish. Chives, mint, parsley or dill all work nicely with the other flavours.

 1 hour 4

- 250g/9oz crème fraîche
- 250ml/9fl oz milk
- zest and juice 1 lemon
- 85g/3oz grated Parmesan
- 2 garlic cloves, crushed
- 140g/5oz broccoli florets
- 100g/4oz frozen soya beans
- 100g/4oz frozen peas
- 100g/4oz mangetout
- 350g/12oz pasta shapes
- handful basil leaves

1 Heat the slow cooker if necessary. Whisk the crème fraîche, milk, lemon zest, Parmesan and garlic together in the slow cooker pot. Stir in the green vegetables and pasta shapes, then cover and cook on High for 30 mins until the veg is just tender and the pasta is cooked.

2 Stir in the lemon juice, some seasoning and the basil leaves and serve.

PER SERVING 734 kcals, fat 36g, saturates 22g, carbs 75g, sugars 9g, fibre 7g, protein 29g, salt 0.5g

Roasted-squash Risotto with Wensleydale

This risotto has a double hit of tasty butternut squash – a creamy, sweet purée cooked with the rice, and crispy, roasted squash chunks scattered over to finish.

 3½ hours   4

- about 1kg/2lb 4oz peeled, deseeded butternut squash, cubed
- 1 onion, chopped
- 1 garlic clove, crushed
- 25g/1oz butter
- 1 litre/1¾ pints hot vegetable stock
- 350g/12oz risotto rice
- 1 tbsp olive oil
- handful pumpkin seeds
- 100g/4oz Wensleydale or vegetarian alternative, crumbled
- small bunch chives, snipped

1 Heat the slow cooker if necessary. Put half the squash, the onion, garlic, butter and 900ml/1½ pints of the stock in the slow cooker pot. Cover and cook on High for 2 hours until the squash is really tender. Mash the squash in the pot or whizz to a purée with a stick blender.

2 Rinse the rice in a sieve until the water runs clear. Drain, then stir into the slow cooker. Cover and cook again on High for 1 hour until the rice is tender and creamy.

3 Meanwhile, heat oven to 200C/180C fan/gas 6. Toss the remaining squash in the oil in a roasting tin and roast for 15–20 mins until tender and golden. With 4–5 mins to go, toss in the pumpkin seeds with a little salt, spread the seeds amongst the squash, then finish roasting.

4 Season the risotto and loosen with the remaining stock if you need to. Serve in shallow bowls, scattering over the roasted squash and pumpkin seeds, crumbled cheese and chives.

PER SERVING 599 kcals, fat 18g, saturates 9g, carbs 93g, sugars 15g, fibre 8g, protein 17g, salt 1.1g

Tomatoes Stuffed with Pesto Rice

Stuffed with spinach, pesto rice and melting mozzarella, these tomatoes make a tasty veggie supper or side.

 2-3 hours 3

- 1 tbsp olive oil, plus extra for drizzling
- 6 large beef tomatoes
- 100g/4oz basmati rice
- 3 tbsp basil pesto
- 100g/4oz grated mozzarella
- 80g bag spinach leaves, roughly chopped
- 400ml/14fl oz hot vegetable stock

1 Heat the slow cooker and oil the base of the pot. Slice the tops off the tomatoes and set aside. Scoop out the insides with a teaspoon, keeping the tomatoes intact. Discard the tomato seeds, but roughly chop the tomato tops. Tip the rice into a bowl, mix with the pesto and season well. Mix in the chopped tomato, three-quarters of the mozzarella, the spinach and some seasoning.

2 Spoon the rice mixture into the tomatoes and pack the stuffed tomatoes tightly into the slow cooker pot. Pour the stock over and around the tomatoes, filling the pot with as much liquid as possible. Drizzle with a little more olive oil and cook on High for 1–2 hours, until the tomatoes are tender and the rice is cooked. Scoop the tomatoes into a baking dish, scatter with the remaining cheese and put under a high grill until melted and golden.

PER SERVING 377 kcals, fat 18g, saturates 6g, carbs 36g, sugars 11g, fibre 6g, protein 13g, salt 1.3g

Tomato & Onion Bake with Goat's Cheese

This dish sounds simple, but is really delicious. Serve with fresh crusty bread for mopping up all the lovely sauce.

 8½ hours 4

- 6 onions, halved (keep root intact)
- 4 garlic cloves, crushed
- 2 tbsp olive oil
- 680ml bottle passata
- 1 tsp caster sugar
- 85g/3oz white breadcrumbs
- 125g log goat's cheese, crumbled
- country bread, to serve

1 Heat the slow cooker if necessary. Put the onions in the slow cooker pot, cut-side down. Mix together the garlic, oil, passata, sugar and some seasoning, and pour over the onions. Cover and cook on Low for 8 hours, or until the onions are tender.

2 Heat a grill and transfer the onions and tomato sauce to a baking dish, if you need to. Sprinkle over the breadcrumbs and goat's cheese, then grill until bubbling and golden.

PER SERVING 346 kcals, fat 15g, saturates 6g, carbs 39g, sugars 19g, fibre 5g, protein 14g, salt 1.1g

Creamy Celery Gratin

This dish works equally well with fish, chicken or pork, or if you add a green salad and a chunk of bread, it would make a great vegetarian main course.

 2½ hours 6

- 2 celery heads, trimmed
- 50g/2oz butter, melted
- 1 onion, thinly sliced
- 2 bay leaves
- 100g/4oz breadcrumbs
- 50g/2oz walnuts, roughly chopped
- 75ml/2½fl oz white wine
- 250ml/9fl oz vegetable or chicken stock
- 100ml/3½fl oz double cream
- 25g/1oz grated Parmesan or vegetarian alternative

1 Heat the slow cooker if necessary. Cut any thick celery sticks in half and trim all of it into thumb-sized lengths. Mix in the slow cooker pot with half the butter, the onion and bay. Cover and cook on High for 2 hours until tender.
2 Meanwhile, mix the remaining butter with the crumbs and walnuts. Set aside.
3 Heat grill to medium. When the celery is tender, tip it into a heatproof dish and stir in the white wine, stock and double cream with some seasoning. Scatter with the breadcrumbs and Parmesan. Grill for 2–3 mins, until the sauce bubbles and breadcrumbs are crisp. Let it sit for 5 mins before serving.

PER SERVING 304 kcals, fat 24g, saturates 11g, carbs 17g, sugars 3g, fibre 2g, protein 7g, salt 0.91g

Cabbage with Beans & Carrots

This all-in-one side dish is clever and delicious, and also versatile enough to be served with a variety of different things. Drop the bacon for a vegetarian version.

 2½–3½ hours 6

- 25g/1oz butter
- 4 rashers smoked streaky bacon, chopped
- 2 carrots, peeled and chopped into small chunks
- 1 Savoy cabbage, quartered, cored and shredded
- 400g can haricot beans, drained and rinsed
- 300ml/½ pint chicken or vegetable stock

1 Heat the slow cooker if necessary. Heat the butter in a pan and fry the bacon until it starts to crisp. Tip into the slow cooker pot with the carrots, cabbage, beans and stock. Cover and cook on High for 2–3 hours until the carrots are tender.
2 Season and serve.

PER SERVING 169 kcals, fat 8g, saturates 3g, carbs15 g, sugars 8g, fibre 7g, protein 10g, salt 1.17g

Red Cabbage with Balsamic Vinegar & Cranberries

Don't just save this for Christmas! You can replace the cranberries with a Bramley apple, if you like, if you can't find the cranberries out of season.

 2½-3½ hours   8

- 3 tbsp olive oil
- 2 large onions, halved and thinly sliced
- 1 tsp ground cloves
- 1 medium red cabbage, quartered, cored and thinly sliced
- 200ml/7fl oz vegetable stock
- 3 tbsp balsamic vinegar
- 100g/4oz soft brown sugar
- 200g/8oz frozen cranberries

1 Heat the slow cooker if necessary. Heat the oil in a large pan. Add the onions and fry, stirring every now and then, for about 10 mins, until they start to caramelise. Stir in the cloves, then add the cabbage, stock, vinegar and sugar with the cranberries.

2 Tip into the slower cooker, cover and cook for 2-3 hours on High until tender. It will keep in the fridge for up to 4 days.

PER SERVING 139 kcals, fat 5g, saturates 1g, carbs 22g, sugars 20g, fibre 4g, protein 3g, salt 0.1g

Sweet Braised Onions

This vegetarian side dish works well with a Sunday lunch. The whole onions are sweetened with balsamic vinegar and maple syrup.

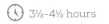 3½–4½ hours 6

- olive oil, for greasing and drizzling
- 12 small red onions
- 1½ tbsp balsamic vinegar
- 2 tbsp maple syrup

1 Heat the slow cooker, if necessary. Cut about 1cm/½in off the top and bottom of each onion and peel off the skin. Nestle the onions in the pot so that they fit snugly together in a single layer.
2 Drizzle over a little oil, the balsamic vinegar, maple syrup and 3 tablespoons water; season. Cover the onions loosely with baking parchment and cook for 3–4 hours until tender.

PER SERVING 89 kcals, fat 3g, saturates none, carbs 14g, sugars 11g, fibre 2g, protein 2g, salt 0.1g

Chapter 6:

PUDDINGS & PRESERVES

Merlot-poached Pears with Vanilla & Cinnamon

Whole pears gently poached in spiced wine makes a dessert that is not too rich, but looks very elegant for a simple dinner party dessert.

 2½ hours   8

- 750ml bottle Merlot or other red wine
- 200g/7oz golden caster sugar
- 2 cinnamon sticks, snapped in half
- 1 vanilla pod, halved lengthways then halved across to make 4 strips
- 8 firm pears, peeled

1 Tip the wine, sugar, cinnamon and vanilla into a pan and heat gently until the sugar dissolves and it is bubbling.

2 Heat the slow cooker if necessary. Check that the pears can stand upright. Trim a thin sliver from the base of the pears if that helps. Put them in the slow cooker and pour in the mulled wine. Cover and cook on low for 2 hours or until a skewer can be pushed into them easily. The pears are likely to float as they cook, so turn them halfway through their poaching time so that they are evenly coloured by the wine.

3 If you want the juice to be more syrupy, remove the pears from the pot with a slotted spoon and pour the liquid into a pan. Boil the juice until reduced in quantity and more syrupy. Pour over the pears, cool, then chill.

PER SERVING 399 kcals, fat none, saturates none, carbs 65g, sugars 65g, fibre 4g, protein 1g, salt 0.1g

Rhubarb & Ginger Syllabub

Using a slow cooker is a great way to cook rhubarb as it's nice and gentle, with no agitation, so the fruit becomes tender without collapsing into mush.

 3 hours, plus cooling   4

- 400g/14oz rhubarb, diced
- thumb-sized piece ginger, peeled and finely chopped
- 75g/2½oz caster sugar
- 100ml/3½fl oz white wine
- 100g/4oz light mascarpone
- 300ml/½ pint double cream
- 50g/2oz icing sugar
- 2 pieces crystallised ginger, finely chopped

1 Heat the slow cooker if necessary. Put the rhubarb, root ginger, sugar and white wine in the pot, cover and cook on Low for 2 hours until the rhubarb is tender. Remove from the slow cooker and set aside to cool.

2 Whisk the mascarpone, double cream and icing sugar to soft peaks. Remove 4 tablespoons of the cooled rhubarb and mash with a fork, then fold into the cream mixture.

3 To serve, divide the rest of the poached rhubarb into four glasses, reserving a bit. Spoon over the cream mixture, then top with a few pieces of crystallised ginger, and the rest of the rhubarb.

PER SERVING 592 kcals, fat 46g, saturates 29g, carbs 36g, sugars 36g, fibre 1g, protein 5g, salt 0.1g

Plum & Amaretti Semifreddo

A ripple of sweet plum purée and chunks of amaretti biscuits turn this Italian ice cream into an all-in-one dessert – just the thing to eat outdoors when the weather is fine.

 5 hours plus cooling and freezing 8

- 450g/1lb ripe purple plums, halved and stoned
- 350g/12oz caster sugar
- 1 tbsp Amaretti liqueur
- 2 large egg whites
- 300ml/½ pint double cream
- 85g/3oz soft amaretti biscuits, roughly broken up

1 Heat the slow cooker if necessary. Put the plums in the pot with 2 tablespoons water, 110g/4oz of the sugar and the liqueur. Cover and cook for 4 hours on Low. Allow to cool slightly, then blitz with a stick blender. Pass through a sieve to remove the plum skins. Allow to cool.

2 Put the remaining sugar in a pan with 150ml/5fl oz water, and dissolve over a low heat. Boil for 5 minutes or until the mixture reaches 120C/250F on a cooking thermometer. Whisk the egg whites until stiff. With the beaters running, carefully pour the sugar mixture onto the egg white, whisking until thick. In another bowl, softly whip the cream, then gently fold in the meringue mixture until smooth, followed by the slow-cooked plum pulp and biscuits.

3 Scrape into a freezable container, cover with cling film and freeze for a few hours or until set. To serve, remove from the freezer 5 mins before scooping into balls.

PER SERVING 435 kcals, fat 22g, saturates 13g, carbs 55g, sugars 54g, fibre 2g, protein 3g, salt 0.1g

Classic Summer Pudding

We can't think of a nicer way to celebrate all the gorgeous berries that are in season in summer than with this delicious pudding.

 2½ hours, plus overnight chilling   6

- 300g/10oz raspberries, plus a few extra to serve
- 225g/8oz blackberries, plus a few extra to serve
- 100g/4oz redcurrants, plus a few extra to serve
- 140g/5oz golden caster sugar, plus a bit extra (optional)
- 400g/14oz strawberries, hulled and quartered
- 400g/14oz brioche loaf, crusts trimmed, sliced into 1cm-thick, long slices along the wrong way of the loaf
- clotted cream or single cream, to serve

1 Heat the slow cooker if necessary. Wash the fruit then place the raspberries, blackberries and redcurrants in the pot with the sugar and 2 tablespoons water. Cover and cook for 1 hour on High.

2 Add the strawberries, cover and cook for 1 hour more. Drain the juice from the fruit, reserving both. Add sugar if necessary.

3 Line a 1.2-litre pudding basin with a double layer of cling film. Trim one brioche slice to fit in the base of the basin. Trim other slices to the correct length to line the sides. Dip the slices into the juice, then use to line the sides. Patch any gaps with the remaining brioche, saving some for the base. Tip in the fruit. Finish with a brioche layer, then pour over any remaining juice. Cover with cling film.

4 Sit a small plate on top and weigh down with two cans. Leave overnight.

5 To serve, unwrap the film, place a serving plate over the pudding, flip it over, remove the basin and peel away the film. Top the pudding with the extra raspberries, blackberries and redcurrants. Serve with clotted or single cream.

PER SERVING 369 kcals, fat 7g, saturates 5g, carbs 68g, sugars 43g, fibre 6g, protein 7g, salt 0.9g

Crème Caramels

Once you have mastered the caramel, these are really easy, as a slow cooker makes an ideal bain-marie for gently cooking the custard.

🕐 3 hours, plus chilling   4

FOR THE CARAMEL
- 100g/4oz caster sugar
- 2 tbsp water

FOR THE CUSTARD
- 300ml/½ pint milk
- 2 large eggs, plus 2 egg yolks
- 85g/3oz caster sugar
- few drops vanilla paste or extract

1 Get out four ramekins. Put the sugar in a small frying pan, preferably non-stick, and add 2 tablespoons water. Heat slowly, stirring gently with a metal spoon until the sugar has dissolved. The base of the pan will no longer feel gritty when you run the spoon over it.

2 Increase the heat under the pan and allow the syrup to bubble. As the water is driven off, the syrup will become thicker. Watch it carefully, without stirring it, until it turns golden at the edges. Swirl the pan to ensure it is evenly coloured and when it is all a rich caramel, pour it into the ramekins.

3 Heat the slow cooker if necessary and put on the kettle. Warm the milk until starting to simmer. Put the eggs and yolks in a bowl with the sugar and whisk lightly together. Gradually whisk in the hot milk, then strain into a clean jug and add the vanilla. Pour into the prepared ramekins and cover each one with foil.

4 Carefully place in the slow cooker and pour boiling water from the kettle into the pot to come halfway up the sides of the ramekins. Cover and cook on Low for 2 hours until the custard is set. Lift out and leave to cool, then chill for at least 4 hours, or overnight.

5 To turn out each caramel, run the point of a sharp knife around the top edge of each ramekin, place a dessert plate on top and invert. Give the ramekin and plate a sharp shake and carefully remove the ramekin.

PER SERVING 267 kcals, fat 7g, saturates 2g, carbs 46g, sugars 46g, fibre none, protein 8g, salt 0.21g

Little Blueberry Puddings with Lemon Sauce

These little puds look deceptively sweet, but they contain a sponge bursting with berries and the sauce is deliciously tangy. Make as a treat for your loved one.

 1½ hours   2

- 50g/2oz softened butter, plus extra for the moulds
- 50g/2oz caster sugar
- 1 egg
- 50g/2oz self-raising flour
- zest 1 lemon, plus 2 tbsp juice
- 4 tbsp blueberries
- crème fraîche or Greek yogurt, to serve

FOR THE SAUCE
- 100g/4oz lemon curd
- 1 tsp cornflour

1 Heat the slow cooker if necessary and put the kettle on. Butter two individual pudding basins or dariole moulds and line the bottoms with circles of baking parchment. Beat the butter, sugar, egg, flour and lemon zest with 1 tablespoon of the juice. Fold in the berries and divide the mixture between the moulds.

2 Sit the moulds in the pot. Pour in boiling water from the kettle to come halfway up the sides. Bake for 1 hour on High until risen and a skewer comes out clean.

3 Meanwhile, make the sauce. Warm the lemon curd in a small pan. Slowly mix the remaining lemon juice into the cornflour until it is a smooth paste, then stir into the lemon curd. Bubble for 1 minute, stirring, until smooth.

4 To serve, carefully run a cutlery knife around the edge of each mould to release. Turn out onto serving dishes and spoon the lemon sauce on top. Eat with a dollop of crème fraîche or yogurt.

PER PUDDING 540 kcals, fat 25g, saturates 13g, carbs 77g, sugars 47g, fibre 1g, protein 7g, salt 0.83g

Schooldays Treacle Sponge

Steamed sponges were made for slow cookers – just check your pudding basin fits in the cooking pot before you start assembling the pudding.

 5 hours    4 generously

- 175g/6oz unsalted butter, softened, plus extra for greasing
- 3 tbsp golden syrup, plus extra for drizzling (optional)
- 1 tbsp fresh white breadcrumbs
- 175g/6oz golden caster sugar
- zest 1 lemon
- 3 eggs, beaten
- 175g/6oz self-raising flour
- 2 tbsp milk
- custard or clotted cream, to serve

1 Heat the slow cooker if necessary. Use a small knob of butter to heavily grease a 1-litre pudding basin. In a small bowl, mix the golden syrup with the breadcrumbs, then tip into the pudding basin.

2 Beat the butter with the sugar and zest until light and fluffy, then add the eggs gradually. Fold in the flour, then finally add the milk.

3 Spoon the mix into the pudding basin. Cover with a double layer of buttered foil and baking paper, making a pleat in the centre to allow the pudding to rise. Tie the foil securely with string, then put in to the slow cooker pot, pouring in enough boiling water from the kettle to come halfway up the sides of the basin. Cover with the lid and cook on High for 4 hours until a skewer poked in comes out clean.

4 Turn out onto a serving dish. Serve with lashings of custard or clotted cream and a little extra golden syrup drizzled over, if you wish.

PER SERVING 763 kcals, fat 43g, saturates 25g, carbs 90g, sugars 56g, fibre 1g, protein 10g, salt 0.71g

Blackberry Queen of Pudding Pots

These puddings are perfect if you have a glut of blackberries. If using wild fruits, taste a few first, gauge how sweet they are, then add more sugar accordingly.

 2 hours   3

- 1 tbsp butter, plus extra for greasing
- 300ml/½ pint full-fat milk
- zest ½ lemon
- 2 eggs, separated
- 100g/4oz golden caster sugar
- 2 individual brioche rolls, sliced
- 75g/2½oz blackberry jam or bramble jelly
- 225g/8oz blackberries

1 Grease three large individual ramekins (about 300ml/ ½ pint each), first checking they can fit in your slow cooker. Heat your slow cooker if necessary. Bring the milk, lemon zest and butter to the boil in a pan, then turn off the heat. Beat the egg yolks with 50g/2oz of the sugar, then strain the hot milk over the egg yolks, beating the mixture constantly.

2 Push the brioche into the ramekins so they are half-full. Pour the custard equally over the brioche, cover the ramekins with foil and put in the slow cooker pot. Pour in enough boiling water to come halfway up the sides of the ramekins. Cover and cook for 1 hour on High until the custard is set, then remove the ramekins from the slow cooker. Mix the jam with the berries, mashing them a little, and divide among the ramekins.

3 Heat grill to medium. Whisk the egg whites to stiff peaks, then gradually whisk in the remaining 50g/2oz sugar until the mixture is stiff again. Swirl meringue over each, then grill until golden.

PER PUDDING 493 kcals, fat 17g, saturates 8g, carbs 78g, sugars 63g, fibre 3g, protein 12g, salt 0.68g

Self-saucing Jaffa Pudding

This pud starts life as an ugly duckling, but don't fear as the hot, watery sauce floats among the batter – once you cook it, you'll end up with something beautiful.

 4 hours 8

- 100g/4oz butter, melted, plus a little extra for greasing
- 250g/9oz self-raising flour
- 140g/5oz caster sugar
- 50g/2oz cocoa powder
- 1 tsp baking powder
- zest and juice 1 orange
- 3 eggs
- 150ml/5fl oz milk
- 100g/4oz orange milk chocolate or milk chocolate, broken into chunks
- vanilla ice cream or single cream, to serve

FOR THE SAUCE
- 200g/7oz light muscovado sugar
- 25g/1oz cocoa powder

1 Remove the pot from the slow cooker and heat the base if necessary. Butter the pot. Put the flour, caster sugar, cocoa, baking powder, orange zest and a pinch of salt in a large mixing bowl. Whisk together the orange juice and any pulp left in the juicer, the eggs, melted butter and milk, then pour on to the dry ingredients and mix together until smooth. Stir in the chocolate chunks and scrape everything into the pot.

2 Mix 300ml/½ pint boiling water from the kettle with the sugar and cocoa for the sauce, then pour this all over the pudding batter – don't worry, it will look very strange at this stage! Return the pot to the slow cooker base, cover and cook on High for 3 hours until the surface looks firm and risen. As you scoop spoonfuls, you should find a rich chocolate sauce underneath the sponge. Eat immediately with vanilla ice cream or single cream.

PER SERVING 522 kcals, fat 21g, saturates 11g, carbs 82g, sugars 54g, fibre 2g, protein 8g, salt 0.86g

Hot Chocolate Mousses

· ·

These are not as rich as most chocolate pots, so the whole family should love them. If you fancy, just cook the whole thing in the slow cooker pot and let everyone dive in.

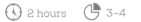 2 hours   3-4  easily halved

- 2 x 58g Mars bars, chopped into pieces
- 50ml/2fl oz milk
- 100g bar dark chocolate
- 3 egg whites
- chocolate shavings, to decorate

1 Heat the slow cooker if necessary. Check you have three or four heatproof pots, cups or mugs that will fit in your slow cooker pot.

2 Put the Mars bars, milk and chocolate in a heavy-based pan. Cook over a very gentle heat, stirring constantly, until the chocolate has melted. Transfer to a bowl and leave to cool for 15 mins, whisking frequently with a wire whisk to blend in any pieces of fudge that rise to the surface to leave a smooth mixture.

3 Whisk the egg whites in a separate bowl until softly peaking. Using a metal spoon, fold a quarter of the whites into the chocolate sauce to lighten it, then fold in the remainder.

4 Divide the mixture among the pots. Cover the top of each with a dome of foil and sit in the slow cooker pot. Pour in enough boiling water to come halfway up the sides of the mousse pots, cover, and cook for 1 hour on High until softly set. Serve topped with chocolate shavings.

· ·

PER SERVING (4) 369 kcals, fat 17g, saturates 9g, carbs 50g, sugars 39g, fibre 1g, protein 8g, salt 0.60g

Apples with Cinnamon Sugar

Spicy apples are the perfect pudding when it's cold outside. Eat these with hot custard, ice cream or single cream.

 2½–3½ hours   6   easily halved

- 50g/2oz natural dried breadcrumbs
- 8 dried ready-to-eat apricots, roughly chopped
- 75g/2½oz sugar
- 1 tsp ground cinnamon
- 75g/2½oz butter, chopped
- zest and juice 1 orange
- 6 large Bramley apples
- custard, ice cream or single cream, to serve

1 Heat the slow cooker if necessary. Mix together the breadcrumbs, apricots, sugar, cinnamon, butter and orange zest.

2 Using an apple corer, remove the centre of each apple, then score the skin across the equator so they don't collapse during cooking.

3 Pack the filling into the apples, then sit them snugly in the slow cooker pot. Mix together the orange juice and 100ml/3½fl oz water, and pour round the apples. Cover and cook on Low for 2–3 hours until the apples are tender. Serve with the pot juices and custard, ice cream or cream.

PER SERVING 246 kcals, fat 11g, saturates 7g, carbs 38g, sugars 32g, fibre 3g, protein 2g, salt 0.26g

Raspberry & Bramble Trifle

This wonderful make-ahead pudding is loosely based on a traditional trifle, but with the added twist of a layer of creamy set custard.

🕐 5 hours, plus chilling overnight   🥧 4-6

- 200g/7oz raspberries, fresh or frozen, plus extra to decorate
- 140g/5oz Madeira cake or any other light sponge, thinly sliced
- 3 tbsp Sherry
- grated zest and juice 1 small orange
- 500ml/18fl oz double cream
- 2 eggs
- 50g/2oz golden caster sugar
- few drops vanilla extract
- 4 tbsp bramble jam or jelly
- 3 shop-bought shortbread biscuits, coarsely crumbled
- icing sugar, to dust

1 Layer the raspberries and cake in a deep heatproof dish that will fit in your slow cooker. Spoon over the Sherry and orange juice.

2 Heat the slow cooker if necessary. Whisk together 400ml/14fl oz of the double cream with the eggs, sugar, orange zest and vanilla extract. Spread the jam over the sponge to cover completely, then slowly pour on the custard mixture. Cover with foil, sit in the slow cooker pot and pour in enough boiling water from the kettle to come halfway up the sides of the dish. Cover and cook on High for 4 hours until the custard is just set with a little wobble. Cool, then cover and chill overnight.

3 To serve, whip the remaining cream until it just holds its shape, then spoon over the custard. Scatter over the raspberries and shortbread, and finish with a dusting of icing sugar.

PER SERVING (6) 873 kcals, fat 70g, saturates 42g, carbs 53g, sugars 36g, fibre 2g, protein 9g, salt 0.58g

Spiced Rice Pudding with Blackberry Compote

This taste delicious whether it is served straight from the slow cooker or chilled.

 4 hours   6

FOR THE RICE
- 200g/8oz brown rice
- 1 tbsp cornflour
- 500ml/18fl oz milk
- 405g can light condensed milk
- 1-2 cinnamon sticks (depending on their length)
- 5 cardamom pods, crushed with a rolling pin
- good grating of nutmeg
- 1 vanilla pod, split and seeds scraped out

FOR THE COMPOTE
- 500g pack frozen blackberries
- 1-2 tbsp agave or maple syrup

1 Heat the slow cooker if necessary. Boil the rice according to pack instructions – don't be tempted to undercook it as it won't continue to cook in the milk.
2 Meanwhile, mix the cornflour with a little of the milk until smooth. Pour the remaining milk into the slow cooker with the condensed milk, spices and vanilla and heat on High while the rice cooks.
3 When the rice is ready, drain it really well and add the milk, stir in the cornflour and stir well. Cook for 20 mins on High, then stir well again and turn down the heat to Low and cook for 3 hours.
4 To make the compote, empty the blackberries into a pan, add the syrup and simmer a few mins until tender. Cool to room temperature before serving with the rice.

PER SERVING 397 kcals, fat 2g, saturates none, carbs 81g, sugars 54g, fibre 5g, protein 13g, salt 0.4g

Blackberry, Apple & Pear Scrumble

Never heard of a scrumble? It's a happy accident created in the *Good Food* kitchen one day. We call it a 'scrumble' as we think it tastes half like a scone, half like crumble!

 4 hours 5

- 3 Bramley apples, peeled, cored and roughly chopped
- 50g/2oz caster sugar
- 3 ripe pears, peeled, cored and roughly chopped
- 225g/8oz blackberries

FOR THE SCRUMBLE
- 250g/9oz plain flour
- 125g/4½oz butter, softened
- 100g/4oz caster sugar
- 4 tbsp milk
- 1 tsp vanilla extract
- granulated sugar, for sprinkling
- vanilla ice cream or double cream, to serve

1 Heat the slow cooker if necessary. Put the apples in the pot with the sugar and 4 tablespoons water. Cover and cook on Low for 2 hours, then stir in the pears and blackberries and cook on Low for 1 hour more. Transfer to a baking dish or five individual pie dishes. If making in advance, the fruit can be chilled for up to 2 days or frozen for up to 3 months.

2 Heat oven to 180C/160C fan/gas 4. To make the scrumble, put the flour, butter, sugar, milk and vanilla in a food processor and pulse until it comes together in a scone-like dough. Drop clumps all over the top of the fruit, then sprinkle generously with granulated sugar. Bake for 40–45 mins until the fruit is bubbling and the scrumble is golden and crisp. Delicious with vanilla ice cream or double cream.

PER SERVING 585 kcals, fat 22g, saturates 13g, carbs 97g, sugars 59g, fibre 6g, protein 6g, salt 0.34g

Apple & Cornflake Pots

Kids will love these clever little pots, made with a few ingredients you should have hanging around in your storecupboard and fruit bowl.

 3–5 hours   4

- 800g/1lb 12oz Bramley apples
- 3 tbsp golden caster sugar
- 2 tbsp golden syrup
- 25g/1oz butter
- 85g/3oz cornflakes
- 200ml/7fl oz low-fat creme fraîche

1 Heat the slow cooker if necessary. Peel, core and thinly slice the apples and put in the slow cooker pot with the caster sugar and 3 tablespoons water. Cover and cook on Low for 2–4 hours until tender.

2 Divide the mixture among four glass tumblers and leave to cool. Meanwhile, heat the golden syrup and butter in a large bowl in the microwave or in a small pan for 1 min to melt. Add the cornflakes and stir well to coat.

3 Top the cooled apple with the crème fraîche, then divide the cornflake mix into the glasses.

PER SERVING 372 kcals, fat 13g, saturates 8g, carbs 60g, sugars 44g, fibre 3g, protein 4g, salt 0.8g

Mandarin-in-the-middle Christmas Pud

This isn't as tricky to make as you might think. Cut the pudding with a serrated knife so that the mandarin stays in place and everyone gets a bit. Serve with cream or brandy butter.

10½ hours, plus soaking and cooling 8-10

- cream or brandy butter, to serve

FOR THE FRUIT
- 140g/5oz each raisins, sultanas and currants
- 140g/5oz glacé cherries, halved
- 50g/2oz blanched almonds, chopped
- 1 medium Bramley apple, peeled, cored and grated to give 175g/6oz flesh
- 50ml/2fl oz orange liqueur
- 150ml/5fl oz medium or sweet Sherry
- zest and juice 1 orange

FOR THE PUDDING
- 140g/5oz cold butter, plus extra, softened, for greasing
- 175g/6oz dark muscovado sugar, plus 2 tbsp for coating the bowl
- 175g/6oz fresh white breadcrumbs
- 140g/5oz self-raising flour
- 1 heaped tsp ground mixed spice
- 2 large eggs, beaten

FOR THE MANDARIN MIDDLE
- 1 firm mandarin or large seedless clementine, about 140g/5oz
- 400g/14oz white granulated sugar
- 2 tbsp orange liqueur

1 First, prepare the fruit. In a large bowl, combine the dried fruit, cherries, almonds and apple with the alcohol, orange juice and zest. Cover with cling film and leave for at least a few hours, or overnight if you can.

2 Next, prepare the mandarin. Put it in a pan, cover with cold water, then cover the surface with a scrunched-up piece of baking parchment. Bring to the boil and cook for 30 mins or until completely tender when poked with a cocktail stick. Remove the mandarin from the water, keeping 300ml/½ pint of the cooking liquid in the pan.

3 Add the sugar to the liquid in the pan and heat gently to dissolve. Poke several holes in the mandarin, then add to the syrup along with the liqueur. Cover with parchment and simmer for 45 mins, turning the mandarin halfway through, until it is a little translucent and a dark orange colour. Leave to cool in the syrup (overnight is fine).

4 To make the pudding, grease a 1.5-litre pudding basin, then scatter over the 2 tablespoons sugar. In a bowl, mix the dry ingredients and a pinch of salt. Coarsely grate the butter and fold in with the dry ingredients, then the eggs.

5 Fill the basin one-third full with the fruit mix, then nestle the mandarin into it. Pack the rest of the mix around and on top of the mandarin and smooth over. You may have some mix left over, depending on the size of the basin.

6 Tear off a sheet of foil and a sheet of baking parchment, both about 30cm/12in long. Butter the parchment and use to cover the foil. Fold a 3cm/1¼in pleat in the middle of the sheets, then put over the pudding, buttered-side down. Tie with string under the lip of the basin, making a handle as you go. Trim the parchment and foil to about 5cm/2in, then tuck the foil around the parchment to seal.

7 To cook the pudding, Heat the slow cooker if necessary. Sit it in the slow cooker pot and pour hot water halfway up the side of the basin and cook on High for 8½ hours. Leave in a cool, dark place to mature.

8 To reheat, steam in the slow cooker, again with water, for 3-4 hours on Low or until thoroughly heated through.

PER SERVING (10) 711 kcals, fat 16g, saturates 8g, carbs 142g, sugars 101g, fibre 3g, protein 8g, salt 0.8

Cranberry Jewelled Mincemeat

Nothing beats homemade mincemeat. To sterilise jars, wash them in very hot, soapy water, rinse well, then leave them in a low oven to dry completely before filling.

8½ hours, plus 24-hour soaking

4 x 330ml/11fl oz jars

- 500g/1lb 2oz mixture of raisins, currants and sultanas (use jumbo or golden sultanas, if you can get them)
- 140g/5oz dried ready-to-eat apricots, chopped
- 85g/3oz dried cranberries
- 85g/3oz mixed peel
- 100ml/3½fl oz brandy
- zest and juice 1 lemon and 1 orange
- 175g/6oz suet
- 100g/4oz fresh or frozen cranberries, roughly chopped
- 200g/7oz soft brown sugar
- 1½ tsp ground cinnamon
- ½ tsp ground nutmeg

1 Tip the dried fruits and mixed peel into a large bowl. Pour over the brandy, citrus zests and juices. Stir, then cover and leave to soak for 24 hours.

2 Heat the slow cooker if necessary. Tip the fruit mixture into the slow cooker pot with the remaining ingredients and stir well. Cover and cook on Low for 8 hours. Pack while hot into sterilised jars. Leave in a cool, dark cupboard for at least a fortnight, or for up to 6 months.

PER 2 TBSP 102 kcals, fat 3g, saturates 2g, carbs 16g, sugars 16g, fibre 1g, protein none, salt none

Seville Orange Marmalade

Buy Seville oranges as soon as you see them in the shops as the season is very short. You can always throw them in the freezer, then defrost them when you have time.

 2 days   8 x 450g/1lb jars

- 1kg/2lb 4oz Seville oranges, well scrubbed and halved
- juice 1 lemon
- 2kg/4lb 8oz granulated sugar

1 Heat the slow cooker if necessary and put a saucer in the freezer. Put the oranges in the slow cooker pot, cover with boiling water and top with an upturned saucer to stop them floating. Cover and cook on Low for 8–10 hours. Leave to cool in the pot overnight.
2 The next day, lift the oranges out of the pot, but don't discard the liquid. Quarter the oranges, scoop out and discard the pips, then thinly slice the quarters.
3 Put the orange slices, cooking liquid, lemon juice and sugar in a very large, wide pan. Gently heat until the sugar has dissolved, then simmer for 20 mins. Spoon a blob of marmalade on to the cold saucer. Leave for a few seconds, then push the marmalade with your finger. If it wrinkles, it's ready. If not, boil for 10 mins more then try again (it can take up to 45 mins).
4 Once you've reached setting point, ladle the marmalade into warm, sterilised jars and seal.

PER TBSP 57 kcals, fat none, saturates none, carbs 15g, sugars 15g, fibre none, protein none, salt none

Apricot & Orange Blossom Conserve

The beauty of homemade jam is that you can make it with a lot less sugar than you'd find in bought versions.

🕐 4 hours, plus overnight standing   🍴 4 X 330ml/11fl oz jars

- 750g/1lb 10oz apricots, halved and stoned, then diced
- 200g/7oz dried ready-to-eat apricots, diced
- 750g/1lb 10oz preserving sugar
- juice 1 lemon
- 1 tbsp orange blossom water
- few knobs of butter (optional)

1 Mix the apricots and the sugar together, cover and leave to stand overnight.
2 Heat the slow cooker if necessary. Tip the syrupy apricots into the pot. Add the lemon juice and orange blossom water, cover and cook on High for 2 hours, then remove the lid, give it a stir and cook uncovered on High for another 1½ hours, stirring often.
3 Stir in knobs of butter, if you like – this will help to dissolve any scum. Leave the jam for 15 mins before ladling into sterilised jars – this allows the fruit to settle so it doesn't sink to the bottom. Will keep in the fridge for 3 weeks or freeze for up to 6 months.

PER TBSP 27 kcals, fat none, saturates none, carbs 6g, sugars 6g, fibre none, protein none, salt none

Spiced Apricot Chutney

Choose your chillies wisely. The fiery little bird's-eye or Scotch bonnet chillies will give far hotter results than medium-sized chillies.

 5-6 hours    about 1.8kg/4lb

- 2 red onions, chopped
- 5cm/2in piece ginger, chopped
- 2 apples, peeled, cored and chopped
- 2 red chillies, roughly chopped seeds and all
- 1kg/2¼lb apricots, stoned and chopped
- 1 tsp each Chinese five-spice powder, paprika, coarsely crushed black peppercorns and salt
- 200g/7oz granulated sugar
- 200ml/8fl oz cider vinegar

1 Heat the slow cooker if necessary. Put the onions, ginger, apples and chillies in a food processor. Blitz until it is all finely chopped, then tip into the slow cooker with the apricots. Add the spices, salt and sugar then cover and cook on High for 2 hours until the apples and apricots are tender.

2 Add the vinegar, cover and cook for another 2–3 hours until pulpy. Pot into warm clean jars and label. Will keep for 3 months.

PER TBSP 24 kcals, fat none, saturates none, carbs 6g, sugars 6g, fibre none, protein none, salt 0.1g

Spicy Plum & Apple Chutney

This chutney is so versatile it won't last long. Eat with cold meats, cheese sandwiches or as an alternative to mango chutney with poppadums.

 4½–5½ hours    4–5 x 450g/1lb jars

- 1 garlic bulb, cloves separated, peeled and sliced
- thumb-sized piece ginger, peeled and thinly shredded
- 2 large onions, thinly sliced
- 1kg/2lb 4oz Bramley apples, peeled, cored and chopped
- 3 star anise
- 1 tsp cumin seeds
- 1 cinnamon stick
- 225g/8oz golden caster sugar
- 1kg/2lb 4oz plums, stoned and quartered
- 250ml/9fl oz cider vinegar

1 Heat the slow cooker if necessary. Mix the garlic, ginger, onions, apples, star anise, cumin seeds, cinnamon, sugar and 1 tablespoon salt together in the slow cooker pot. Cover and cook for 2 hours on High until the apples are tender.

2 Stir in the plums and vinegar, cover and cook for another 2–3 hours on High until pulpy. Stir the chutney every now and then while it's cooking.

3 Discard the cinnamon stick and star anise before ladling the chutney into sterilised jars.

PER TBSP 38 kcals, fat none, saturates none, carbs 10g, sugars 9g, fibre 1g, protein none, salt 0.22g

Pineapple, Fig & Ginger Chutney

To sterilise your jars, wash them in very hot, soapy water and leave to drain. Once dry, put them in the oven at 160C/140C fan/gas 3 for 10 mins before using.

 4½–5½ hours   about 1.3kg/3lb

- 1 large pineapple (about 1kg/2lb 4oz) or 400g/14oz prepared pineapple, roughly chopped
- 500g/1lb 2oz Bramley apples, peeled, cored and finely chopped
- 5cm/2in piece ginger, finely chopped
- 1 red onion, finely chopped
- 140g/5oz dried ready-to-eat figs, chopped
- 2 tsp black mustard seeds
- ½ tsp freshly grated nutmeg
- 200g/7oz light muscovado sugar
- 250ml/9fl oz cider vinegar

1 Heat the slow cooker if necessary. Tip the pineapple into a food processor, then pulse until finely chopped. Tip into the slow cooker pot with the apples, ginger, onion, figs, spices, sugar and 2 teaspoons salt. Cover and cook for 2 hours on High until the apples are tender.

2 Add the vinegar, cover and cook for another 2–3 hours on High until pulpy. Stir the chutney every now and then while it's cooking. Pot into warm sterilised jars, seal and label. Will keep for 3 months.

PER TBSP 44 kcals, fat none, saturates none, carbs 11g, sugars 11g, fibre 1g, protein none, salt 0.21g

Corn Relish

This is a great summer chutney served with hot dogs, burgers or pork chops. Make this when corn cobs are cheap, sweet and plentiful.

 2½–3½ hours    1 x 350g/12oz jar

- 1 tsp vegetable oil
- 1 shallot, finely chopped
- 200–250g/7–9oz fresh sweetcorn (about 2 cobs)
- 1 red chilli, deseeded and finely chopped
- 50ml/2fl oz cider vinegar
- 25g/1oz caster sugar
- ½ tsp dry mustard powder
- handful coriander leaves, finely chopped (optional)

1 Heat the slow cooker if necessary. Mix all the ingredients in the pot – except the coriander, if using – along with ½ teaspoon salt. Cover and cook on High for 2 hours for a relish with a crunch, or for 3 hours if you want it softer.

2 Add the coriander, if using, and leave to cool. Will keep for 1-2 weeks in the fridge in jars.

PER TBSP 24 kcals, fat 1g, saturates none, carbs 4g, sugars 2g, fibre none, protein 1g, salt 0.18g

Tomato & Chilli Harissa

If you've grown more tomatoes and chillies than you can eat, turn them into this Middle Eastern spice paste. Use it in marinades, Moroccan tagines, dips and soups.

 4-5 hours  1 x 350g/12oz jar

- 1 tsp each caraway seeds and coriander seeds
- ½ tsp cumin seeds
- 100ml/4fl oz olive oil, plus a little extra
- 4 garlic cloves, peeled but kept whole
- 1 tsp smoked paprika
- 500g/1lb 2oz tomatoes, deseeded and chopped
- 3 red chillies, deseeded (use more chillies and leave the seeds in if you like it very fiery)
- 1 tsp rose water (optional)

1 Heat the spice seeds in a dry pan until lightly toasted and aromatic, then lightly crush using a pestle and mortar.

2 Heat the slow cooker if necessary. Mix the oil, garlic, toasted spices, paprika, tomatoes and chillies in the pot. Cover and cook on High for 2 hours until the tomatoes are softened and pulpy. Remove the lid and cook for 1–2 hours more, stirring occasionally, until tender and thickened.

3 Remove from the heat, add the rose water, if using, then blitz with a stick blender or pulse in a food processor to make a rough paste. Spoon into a sterilised jar and pour a little oil on the surface to cover it completely. Will keep in the fridge for several months if you cover the surface with oil after each use.

PER TBSP 34 kcals, fat 3g, saturates 1g, carbs 1g, sugars 1g, fibre none, protein none, salt none

Homemade Tomato Sauce

There's nothing quite like home made, and this posh tomato sauce will perk up bacon sandwiches, fish and chips and beef burgers.

 4–5 hours    2 x 200ml/7fl oz bottles

- 1 tbsp olive oil
- 2 onions, chopped
- 1 thumb-sized piece ginger, finely chopped or grated
- 2 garlic cloves, crushed
- 1 red chilli, deseeded and finely chopped
- 800g/1lb 12oz tomatoes, briefly whizzed in a food processor or finely chopped
- 100g/4oz dark soft brown sugar
- 100ml/3½fl oz red wine vinegar
- 2 tbsp tomato purée
- ½ tsp coriander seeds

1 Heat the slow cooker if necessary. Fry the oil and onions together until really soft. Tip into the slow cooker pot and add all the remaining ingredients. Cover and cook for 2 hours on High. Remove the lid and cook for 1–2 hours more, stirring occasionally until saucy.

2 Cool slightly, then whizz in a blender or food-processor until smooth. If the sauce is a bit thick for your liking, stir in a dribble of boiling water. Push through a sieve, then funnel into a sterilised bottle or jar while still hot. Cool completely before serving. Will keep for 3 months in the fridge.

PER TBSP 28 kcals, fat 1g, saturates none, carbs 6g, sugars 6g, fibre 1g, protein none, salt 0.02g

Index

··

aioli with tender summer squid 206
amaretti semifreddo & plum 272
apple
   apple & cornflake pots 296
   apple spice tea loaf 64
   apples with cinnamon sugar 288
   blackberry, apple & pear
      scrumble 294
   curried lentil, parsnip & apple
      soup 30
   herby pressed ham with spiced
      apple compote 40
   Normandy pork with apples &
      cider 186
   spicy plum & apple chutney 308
apricot
   apricot & orange blossom
      conserve 304
   smoky aubergine tagine with
      lemon & apricots 232
   spiced apricot chutney 306
aubergine tagine with lemon &
   apricots 232

bacon
   big-batch bolognese 66
   chicken, bacon & potato stew 112
   pot-roast pheasant with cider &
      bacon 198
   slow-cooked Irish stew 100
   walker's wild mushroom, bacon
      & barley broth 34
banana salsa with jerk pulled pork
   140
barley
   slow-cooked Irish stew 100
   walker's wild mushroom, bacon
      & barley broth 34
bass
   sea bass & seafood Italian
      one-pot 208
   sea bass with black bean sauce
      210
beans
   cabbage with beans & carrots 260
   chicken, butter bean & pepper
      stew 78

creamy black dhal with
   toppings 240
Greek butter bean & tomato
   stew 226
meatball stroganoff 74
smoky pork & Boston beans
   one-pot 76
beef
   beef & stout stew with carrots 168
   beef in red wine with melting
      onions 120
   big-batch bolognese 66
   chilli con carne 70
   Chinese braised beef with
      ginger 176
   cottage pie 68
   meatball stroganoff 74
   minced beef & sweet-potato
      stew 102
   pork & beef chilli with lemon
      pancetta 170
   slow-cooked beetroot & beef
      curry 152
   Thai beef curry 150
beetroot, slow-cooked, & beef
   curry 152
black beans
   black bean chilli 224
   sea bass with black bean sauce
      210
blackberry
   blackberry, apple & pear
      scrumble 294
   blackberry queen of pudding
      pots 282
   spiced rice pudding with
      blackberry compote 292
blueberry puddings with lemon
   sauce 278
bolognese, big-batch 66
bramble trifle & baked raspberry 290
broccoli soup with goat's cheese
   croutons 36

cabbage
   cabbage with beans & carrots 260
   red cabbage with balsamic

vinegar & cranberries 262
caramel, crème 276
carrot
   cabbage with beans & carrots 260
   carrot & coriander soup 32
   spiced carrot & lentil soup 14
cauliflower
   cauliflower & tomato curry 158
   cauliflower cheese & spinach
      pasta bakes 234
cheese
   broccoli soup with goat's
      cheese croutons 36
   cauliflower cheese & spinach
      pasta bakes 234
   courgette, potato & cheddar
      soup 22
   creamy celery gratin 258
   easy cheese fondue 52
   pesto & mozzarella-stuffed
      mushrooms 46
   roasted squash risotto with
      Wensleydale 252
   spinach-baked eggs with
      parmesan & tomato toasts 48
   tomato & onion bake with
      goat's cheese 256
   veg & cheesy rice bake 244
chestnut casserole & venison
   sausage 202
chicken
   Andalusian-style chicken 164
   Cape Malay chicken curry with
      yellow rice 136
   chicken & red wine casserole
      with herby dumplings 116
   chicken arrabbiata 118
   chicken, bacon & potato stew 112
   chicken, butter bean & pepper
      stew 78
   chicken, leek & parsley pie 86
   chicken with sweet wine & garlic
      166
   easy one-pot chicken 88
   light chicken korma 154
   Moroccan harira & chicken
      soup 8

one-pot chicken with chorizo &
new potatoes 114
pesto-chicken stew with cheesy
dumplings 82
poule au pot 80
roast chicken soup 10
salsa chicken peppers 90
saucy chicken & spring
vegetables 94
spicy African chicken & peanut
stew 138
summer roast chicken 92
sweet & sour chicken adobo 144
Thai chicken soup 20
chickpea
chorizo, pork belly & chickpea
casserole 126
summer vegetables & chickpeas
230
vegetable couscous with
chickpeas & preserved
lemons 242
chilli
chilli con carne 70
pork & beef chilli with lemon
pancetta 170
tomato & chilli harissa 314
chocolate
hot chocolate mousses 286
self-saucing jaffa pudding 284
chorizo
chorizo, pork belly & chickpea
casserole 126
one-pot chicken with chorizo &
new potatoes 114
squash & chorizo pot pies 84
cider
Normandy pork with apples &
cider 186
pot-roast pheasant with cider &
bacon 198
slow-braised pork shoulder with
cider & parsnips 128
coconut
Goan prawn & coconut curry
with cumin rice 160
spiced coconut porridge with
cranberry & orange compote
62
coriander & carrot soup 32
courgette, potato & cheddar soup
22
couscous, vegetable, with
chickpeas & preserved
lemons 242
crab-stuffed tomatoes 54

cranberry
cranberry jewelled mincemeat
300
red cabbage with balsamic
vinegar & cranberries 262
curries 148, 150, 152, 158, 160

dhal, creamy black, with toppings
240
duck
Chinese roast duck with
pancakes 44
duck, apricot & pine nut pastilla
194
French duck confit 196
Venetian duck ragu 192

eggs
creamy smoked haddock
kedgeree 106
spinach-baked eggs with
parmesan & tomato toasts 48

fig, pineapple & ginger chutney 310
fish, see also bass, crab, haddock,
salmon, squid
easy paella 108
fish mappas 212
rich paprika seafood bowl 204
fruit
classic summer pudding 274

ginger
Chinese braised beef with
ginger 176
ginger-beer & tangerine-glazed
ham 188
pineapple, fig & ginger chutney
310
rhubarb & ginger syllabub 270

haddock
creamy smoked haddock
kedgeree 106
sweetcorn & smoked haddock
chowder 18
ham
ginger-beer & tangerine-glazed
ham 188
herby pressed ham with spiced
apple compote 40
meatball stroganoff 74
smoky pork & Boston beans
one-pot 76
split pea & green pea smoked-
ham soup

harira, Moroccan, & chicken soup 8
hotpot 98, 124, 146

kedgeree 106
korma 154

lamb
braised shoulder of lamb with
jewelled stuffing 182
lamb & dauphinoise hotpot 124
Lancashire hotpot 98
shepherd's pie with lamb's liver
180
slow-cooked Irish stew 100
sticky spiced lamb shanks 134
Turkish lamb pilaf 178
leek
chicken, leek & parsley pie 86
winter leek & potato soup 12
lemon
little blueberry puddings with
lemon sauce 278
pasta with creamy greens &
lemon 250
pork & beef chilli with lemon &
pancetta 170
smoky aubergine tagine with
lemon & apricots 232
lentil
creamy black dhal with
toppings 240
curried lentil, parsnip & apple
soup 30
lentil ragout 238
spiced carrot & lentil soup 14

mandarin-in-the-middle Christmas
pud 298
marmalade, Seville orange 302
mincemeat, cranberry jewelled
300
mushroom
big-batch bolognese 66
meatball stroganoff 74
mushroom, shallot & squash pie
246
pesto & mozzarella-stuffed
mushrooms 46
spicy spaghetti with garlic
mushrooms 248
walker's wild mushroom, bacon
& barley broth 34
mussels
creamy spiced mussels 56
sea bass & seafood Italian
one-pot 208

onion
  sweet braised onions 264
  tomato & onion bake with
    goat's cheese 256
orange, Seville, marmalade 302
orange blossom & apricot
  conserve 304
ox cheek, braised wellingtons, with
  peppercorn gravy 174
oxtail, braised with basil dumplings
  122

pancetta, lemon, with pork & beef
  chilli 170
parsnip
  curried lentil, parsnip & apple
    soup 30
  parsnip soup with parsley
    cream 26
  slow-braised pork shoulder with
    cider & parsnips 128
pasta
  big-batch bolognese 66
  cauliflower cheese & spinach
    pasta bakes 234
  chicken arrabbiata 118
  lentil ragout 238
  macaroni cheese 218
  pasta with creamy greens &
    lemon 250
  spicy spaghetti with garlic
    mushrooms 248
  turkey pasta bake 72
pea
  pea risotto 50
  pea & watercress soup 28
  split pea & green pea smoked-
    ham soup 18
pear
  blackberry, apple & pear
    scrumble 294
  merlot-poached pears with
    vanilla & cinnamon 268
peppers
  chicken, butter bean & pepper
    stew 78
  salsa chicken peppers 90
pheasant, pot-roast, with cider &
  bacon 198
pineapple
  pineapple, fig & ginger chutney
    310
  sticky pork & pineapple hotpot 146
plum
  braised pork with plums 142
  plum & amaretti semifreddo 272

spicy plum & apple chutney 308
pollock
  fish mappas 212
pork, see also bacon, ham
  BBQ pulled pork 172
  braised pork with plums 142
  Brazilian pork stew with corn
    dumplings 132
  chorizo, pork belly & chickpea
    casserole 126
  country terrine with black
    pepper & thyme 42
  Italian sausage stew with
    rosemary-garlic mash 190
  jerk pulled pork with banana
    salsa 140
  meatball stroganoff 74
  Normandy pork with apples &
    cider 186
  pork & beef chilli with lemon
    pancetta 170
  slow-braised pork shoulder with
    cider & parsnips 128
  smoky pork & Boston beans
    one-pot 76
  stickiest-ever BBQ ribs 96
  sticky pork & pineapple hotpot 146
  sweet pork belly with
    Vietnamese-style salad &
    smashed peanuts 184
porridge, spiced coconut, with
  cranberry & orange
  compote 62
prawns
  Goan prawn & coconut curry
    with cumin rice 160
  hot & sour broth with prawns 24

raspberry, baked, & bramble trifle
  290
rhubarb & ginger syllabub 270
rice pudding, spiced, with
  blackberry compote 292

salmon curry, red Thai, 148
shallot, mushroom & squash pie 246
spinach
  cauliflower cheese & spinach
    pasta bakes 234
  spinach-baked eggs with
    parmesan & tomato toasts 48
  sweet potato & spinach bake 238
squash
  mushroom, shallot & squash pie
    246
  roasted squash risotto with

Wensleydale 252
  squash & chorizo pot pies 84
  squash & venison tagine 130
squid
  sea bass & seafood Italian
    one-pot 208
  tender summer squid with aioli 206
sweetcorn
  corn relish 312
  sweetcorn & smoked haddock
    chowder 18
sweet potato
  minced beef & sweet-potato
    stew 102
  sweet potato & spinach bake 236

tomato (passata)
  cauliflower & tomato curry 158
  crab-stuffed tomatoes 54
  creamy tomato soup 38
  Greek butter bean & tomato
    stew 226
  homemade tomato sauce 316
  spinach-baked eggs with
    parmesan & tomato toasts 48
  tomato & chilli harissa 314
  tomato & onion bake with
    goat's cheese 256
  tomatoes stuffed with pesto rice
    254
treacle sponge 280
turkey pasta bake 72

vegetables
  golden veggie shepherd's pie 20
  Italian vegetable bake 216
  saucy chicken & spring
    vegetables 94
  summer vegetables & chickpeas
    230
  veg & cheesy rice bake 244
  vegetable couscous with
    chickpeas & preserved lemons
    242
  veggie moussaka 222
  winter vegetable curry with
    mango raita 156

venison
  squash & venison tagine 130
  steamed venison & short
    pudding 200
  venison sausage & chestnut
    casserole 202

watercress & pea soup 28

An Introduction to
the Properties of
Engineering Materials